N. T. WRIGHT

small faith
GREAT GOD

Biblical Faith for Today's Christians

SECOND EDITION

An imprint of InterVarsity Press
Downers Grove, Illinois

InterVarsity Press
P.O. Box 1400, Downers Grove, IL 60515-1426
World Wide Web: www.ivpress.com
E-mail: email@ivpress.com

InterVarsity Press® is the book-publishing division of InterVarsity Christian Fellowship/USA®, a movement of students and faculty active on campus at hundreds of universities, colleges and schools of nursing in the United States of America, and a member movement of the International Fellowship of Evangelical Students. For information about local and regional activities, write Public Relations Dept., InterVarsity Christian Fellowship/USA, 6400 Schroeder Rd., P.O. Box 7895, Madison, WI 53707-7895, or visit the IVCF website at <www.intervarsity.org>.

Design: Cindy Kiple
Images: Aleksandar Kolundzija/iStockphoto

ISBN 978-0-8308-3833-2

Printed in Canada ∞

Library of Congress Cataloging-in-Publication Data

Wright, N. T. (Nicholas Thomas)
 Small faith—great God: biblical faith for today's Christians / N.T.
Wright—Rev. and updated ed.
  p. cm.
 Includes bibliographical references and index.
 ISBN 978-0-8308-3833-2 (cloth: alk. paper)
 1. Faith—Biblical teaching. 2. Christian life—Anglican authors.
I. Title.
 BS680.F27W75 2010
 234'.23—dc22

                                                                        2010019899

P	18	17	16	15	14	13	12	11	10	9	8	7	6	5	4	3	2	1
Y	25	24	23	22	21	20	19	18	17	16	15	14	13	12	11	10		

For Keith and Margaret Weston

CONTENTS

PREFACE TO
THE SECOND EDITION

I WAS NERVOUS ABOUT REPUBLISHING these studies, which started out as sermons in and around Oxford. I was still in my early twenties when the first of them was preached— chapter five in this book, preached on Trinity Sunday 1972 in St. Ebbe's Church—and the thought of revisiting after forty years the things I had been trying to say, and the way I had been trying to say them, was somewhat daunting. A bit like looking at old photographs: Did we really have those hairstyles? Those clothes? Those cars?

Well, yes, we did. I had something of that sense in rereading these sermons. We thought they were all right at the time, of course—the hair, the clothes, the cars and the sermons— even though they now feel in some respects embarrassingly dated. But I was also surprised to discover that quite a few themes which I had thought were more recent additions to my thinking were already there in embryo. I think, for instance, of the discussion of hypocrisy in chapter ten, which goes closely with my book *After You Believe*. There are several other connections which the curious reader of my work might tease out.

But what I was really glad to discover was not only that I substantially agreed with so much of what I had written all those years ago, but also that a wealth of memories came flooding back: people and occasions, friends and family, the support and encouragement of so many as I started out on the long and winding journey of ministry, of studying the Bible and trying to preach from it. I have mentioned St. Ebbe's Church in Oxford; the other place which heard many of these sermons was Merton College Chapel. Keith Weston, the then rector of St. Ebbes, and Mark Everitt, the then chaplain of Merton, were and are very different people, from very different sections of the Church of England. But both gave me the space to explore new ideas and preach about them. That was a great gift. The fact that it's hard to tell, without some other clue, which sermons were preached in which of the two places indicates, I hope, that fresh biblical exposition belongs to the whole church, not to one party or strand.

There are, of course, several features which do indeed look decidedly dated. Nobody supposed in those days that spanking naughty children constituted "child abuse." And I realize, in particular, that my more recent work on the ultimate Christian hope (as in *The Resurrection of the Son of God* and *Surprised by Hope*) needs to be brought to bear on what I say about "heaven," especially in chapter nine and also, for instance, the final chapter of this book (which I remember writing frantically one summer Sunday in Oxford, after hours of writer's block and urgent prayer, before cycling the two miles to Merton College at breakneck speed, arriving just in time for the service). And I have changed my mind about some things: for instance, analysis of the Pharisees in chapter ten, and the place of Paul's imprisonment in chapter eleven.

But I don't think that the emphasis I would now place on new heavens and new earth (rather than just "heaven") makes much difference to the main thrust of the book. The greatness of God the Creator and Redeemer is what matters. Our little faith grasps now this aspect of his greatness, now that. But it is God himself who counts, not our perceptions or understanding of him, not our faith or our rhetoric or our pilgrimage. I hope and pray that this little book, period piece though it be, will still be able to make that point clear.

part one

FAITH IN A GREAT GOD

1

ENTHRONED IN
HEAVENLY SPLENDOR

"I'D LOVE TO BE A FLY ON THE WALL when that happens!"
So we often say, wishing we could be present at some important meeting or could listen in on some high-level discussion.
Well, we're going to begin this book by becoming flies on the
wall at a scene of great beauty, as well as of great significance
for our understanding of God, of the world and of ourselves.
Like all eavesdroppers, we may be in for a few surprises.

The scene is set for us in the fourth and fifth chapters of the
book of Revelation. If you find the picture confusing to begin
with, you are not alone. All these beasts and crowns and thunder and lightning—you may be tempted to dismiss the whole
thing as so much incomprehensible mumbo jumbo. Please
don't. Revelation isn't mumbo jumbo: it's written in symbols,
and once you understand the symbols most of the problems
disappear. Of course, nobody understands them all, or per-

fectly, but we can make a reasonable job of it.

With language like this we have to stop thinking of it as if it were a photograph of heaven—as though such a thing were possible! Revelation is more like a map: and a map, once we learn the symbols it uses, is actually of more use to us than an aerial photograph would be. We don't imagine for a moment that when we are climbing a hill we will actually *see* the contour lines as we cross them on the map. And if we are driving down a road and turn off on a side road, the road is unlikely to change color the way it does on the map. But contours and road colors are not useless. They tell us important facts about where we are going. We would be lost without them.

We would certainly be lost—for good—without the facts presented in Revelation 4–5: our problem is to work out what those facts are. If the language is symbolic, like the symbols on a map, then we shouldn't try to imagine the scene literally— the Lion which is also a lamb, with seven horns and seven eyes, stretches our imagination as far as it will go, and probably further. What we have to do is to get into John's mind and understand what he was wanting to say by these symbols. Then we shall be able to join him, like flies on the wall, in seeing the invisible and hearing things our human ears couldn't normally hear.

The first thing we see sets the context for everything that is to come. There before me, says John, was a throne, with someone sitting on it. Someone. Not even with symbols does John attempt to describe God who sits on the throne: but the fact that he is enthroned tells us the first important thing about him. He is the King. He is sovereign. And the sight is not just awe-inspiring: it is positively beautiful, surrounded by many-colored jewels and capped by the rainbow, which John mentions to remind us that this is the same God as revealed to Noah and Ezekiel—the God who makes loving and gracious promises and keeps them.

With the beauty and the love goes great power and majesty. God's throne, surrounded by the twenty-four thrones of the elders, sends out flashes of lightning and peals of thunder. In a few short sentences John has let us in on a picture of God so big and terrible that we are forced to ask—is this really the God we believe in? Or is the God of the Bible not bigger and greater than most of our usual pictures of God? This book is about faith: and the way to faith is always down the road of an enlarged view of God, a view constantly checked and revised in the light of the Bible. Without this, the God we worship shrinks into an idol, formed by our own imagination. Faith in an idol is no faith worth having.

The creatures in the scene John is describing, however, were not worshiping an idol. We can always tell. Idol worshipers may be concerned with many things, but they are never thinking about holiness. Instead, they are either not thinking about ethical standards at all—since an idol is impersonal and therefore not bothered about such things—or they are following a hollow asceticism, which is the outward form of holiness minus the inner joy that dwells at the heart of the true God. But the four living creatures think of nothing but holiness— because they think of nothing but God.

Who are the creatures? In John's symbolism, they represent the world of creation—nature, animals, plants. This is the song the sun sings as it rises. This is what trees sing as their leaves change color. This is what the penguins sing as they march around the ice. Fanciful? Not a bit of it. God's creation, sustained by him from moment to moment, is full of his glory, if only we had eyes to see it.

We can have eyes to see it. The beasts are not alone in their singing. As creation sings God's praise, so the song is continually taken up by the twenty-four elders. And who are they? The church, the people of God: twelve to stand for the twelve tribes in the Old Testament, and twelve to stand for the successors of the apostles, the church in the New Testament era. The church is a family of priests, summing up the praises of creation in their own praise. But their praise goes beyond that of creation. Nature simply praises God: redeemed humans understand why God ought to be praised. You are *worthy*, sing the elders, to receive glory and honor and power. It is one of the signs of life in the people of God that they find themselves echoing that song.

There is another song which the redeemed people sing, and it comes in Revelation 5. So far in our eavesdropping we have seen a great vision of God. Now we hear something which comes closer and touches us personally. In the right hand of the figure on the throne is a sealed scroll. God holds out the book which contains his perfect plan for the righteous and holy ruling of his world. And, just as God is not described directly, so he does not act directly. God, it appears, has purposed that his will should be carried out by a person or people other than himself. And that's the problem. Who on earth can be worthy to carry out God's will, to act as his right-hand man in ruling the world? For a minute it looks as though, bound by his own decree, God will never vindicate truth and justice—as though the whole world is going to turn out meaningless and futile. No wonder John burst into tears.

The answer to the problem is close at hand, and in fact this moment is the climax of the whole sequence of events so far. There is someone who can open the book. If we found the vision of God bewildering yet awe-inspiring, the same is going to be true of this picture of Jesus Christ. He is the Lion of Judah—the sovereign one from the tribe which God chose out of his chosen people. He is the Root of David—the stock from which came the man after God's own heart. And he has triumphed. We turn with John, expecting to see a kingly figure ready to sweep all God's enemies out of the way and to rule the world with a rod of iron. And we see—a lamb. Worse, a lamb that has been killed. Yet, although it has been killed, this lamb is alive again, and now has been given complete power and authority (the seven horns), and the rule over the spirits who rule the world. Why? How does the picture even begin to make sense?

It makes sense very simply. The Lion of Judah won the victory by *being* the lamb who was sacrificed: because the enemies that were to be defeated were sin (the thing which meant that no one else was worthy to open the book) and death, which follows from sin. And the Lion defeated death by dying as the lamb. He died to take away sin, taking the full weight of evil on himself, dying in refusing to submit to it. He, and he alone, is worthy.

Now at this point we have reached the eavesdropper's dilemma. What we are now hearing sounds suspiciously as though it is going to involve us: and that might not be such fun as just being a fly on the wall. Yet if we decide to go on listening nonetheless, what we hear will turn out to be for our benefit. Listen to the song which the beasts and elders now sing:

> You are worthy to take the scroll
>> and to open its seals,
> because you were slain,
>> and with your blood you purchased men for God
>> from every tribe and language and people and nation.
> You have made them to be a kingdom and priests to serve
>> our God,
>> and they will reign on the earth.
>> (Revelation 5:9-10 NIV)

This song is about what Christ, the Lion of Judah, did. And we, the eavesdroppers, discover that it's about *us*. Here are truths about us earthlings which are sung with joy by the inhabitants of heaven. We can summarize them like this.

First, the depth of the gospel. Christ purchased humans for God. That is, he came into the slave market where his people were standing in chains, and he paid the cost of setting them free. This isn't something he has to do over and over again. It's in the past: it's a completed action.

Second, the breadth of the gospel. There is no nation or people—no tribe or language—from which Christ did not buy himself people for his own possession. That is why, over against the exclusivism that implied that a person had to be born a Jew in order to qualify, the early church stressed (and we should not forget) that the achievement of Christ knows no barriers of color or class, of birth or social status.

Third, the purpose of the gospel. Christ purchased humans first and foremost for *God*, to be kings and priests to serve him. Realize the full impact of this. When Christ bought us at the cost of his own blood, it wasn't first and foremost for our happiness—though to be saved by him will mean happiness itself. He bought us for God. It was on commission from the Father that the Son came down to the slave market that day. He set us free to be—freemen? Just one grade up from slaves? Certainly not. Nothing mealy-mouthed about this freedom: we are to be kings, to share in God's work of ruling the world. And we are to be priests, representing the whole of creation to God, summing up its praises in our own.

This dual role (kings and priests) ties in exactly with the dual role of Christ, as the regal lion and the sacrificial lamb. This is just what we should expect. We are given these tasks simply and solely in virtue of what he has done. The eavesdroppers are not just hearing themselves mentioned, they are listening in on the forming and celebrating of plans that are going to make them spiritual millionaires. Here is God the Almighty planning his purposes; here is the Lion of Judah, who has died as the sacrificial lamb; here are the re-

deemed people praising this achievement; and we find ourselves caught up in it all, caught up in the amazing sweep of
God's grace.

Which is why the eavesdropping must come to an end. We
must come out from our hiding and admit that we have heard
what has been going on. After all, the whole of creation is
praising God the almighty Maker—the whole of the church is
praising Christ the sovereign Redeemer—and are we going to
remain silent? This applies whether we have been Christians
for fifty years or for five minutes—and it applies equally well
to those who have never given the matter a thought before.
God's word through John is quite clear: our lives are to be
lived in the light of the praise of heaven. This isn't a half-
hearted or dreary suggestion. Being a Christian is not a matter
of vague ideals and wishy-washy ideas. It is a matter of thousands upon thousands of God's ransomed people singing un-
inhibitedly the song of their deliverance.

> Worthy is the Lamb that was slaughtered,
> to receive power and wealth and wisdom and might
> and honor and glory and blessing! (Revelation 5:12)

That is the context in which all Christian living takes place.
Christian faith—biblical faith—is not a matter of putting a
brave face on things and trying our best. It is a matter of looking away from ourself and seeing the world as God sees it, as
it really is. In the real world every creature in heaven and on
earth and under the earth and in the sea, and all that is in
them, is singing,

To the one seated on the throne and to the Lamb
be blessing and honor and glory and might,
forever and ever! (Revelation 5:13)

Creation is saying "Amen." The church bows down and worships. These are the facts. The question of faith is whether we stop eavesdropping and join in the song.

2

POWER TO THE FAINT

WE ARE NOW IN A POSITION TO close in on the central theme of the book, which will occupy us in chapter three. If we can anticipate what we are going to say there, we could put it like this: faith in the Bible is always determined by its object. Or, if you like, what matters is not so much the faith itself as what it is faith *in*. Faith, as we shall see, is like a window. It is not there because we happen to want one wall of the room to be made of glass. It is there for the sake of what we can see through it—and in order to let light into the room.

We thought in chapter one about God as the Creator God, the one who made the world in the first place and has now begun the task of remaking it. We're now going to look at a passage where this truth about God is used as the basis of his people's faith. But it isn't a question of the people themselves having particularly special faith. Indeed, they are rather a sorry lot. The point is simply that they are the people of the great God.

The passage in question is one which most of us are so familiar with that we don't think clearly about it any more. It is one which would figure prominently on many a Christian's list of favorite texts. When we read it again it isn't surprising:

> Those who wait for the LORD shall renew their strength,
> they shall mount up with wings like eagles,
> they shall run and not be weary,
> they shall walk and not faint. (Isaiah 40:31)

Marvelous stuff, whether we read it as poetry or as theology. Just the sort of thing we all need from time to time. But wait. That is the *end* of the chapter. Nor is that an accident: this splendid encouraging verse is in fact built four-square upon things the prophet has been saying before. One of the most characteristic pitfalls of much modern Christianity is the attempt to get the results without the working—trying to jump straight to the helpful bit at the end without seeing that we can only get there properly if we follow what has already been said. The Bible is not just a collection of helpful texts: it is a real book, or rather a collection of real books, and the lines of thought that run right through chapters or whole books are often much more important than any of the individual verses on the way. This is certainly true here. The only way to make sure we mount up with wings as eagles is to make sure it really is the Lord that we are waiting on. We cannot take that for granted. That is why this part of Isaiah was written.

Isaiah was writing for people who were trying to face the fact of the exile God had threatened as the punishment on his people for their sin and idolatry. And among the many things he tells the people about their true God, the God who is so unlike the imaginary gods they have been worshiping, is just this: Yahweh, the LORD, the God of Israel, is the sovereign Creator God. He is unique. There is no other God like him. It is a simple enough picture, but just look at the colors in which it is painted. Read Isaiah 40:12-26. Yahweh, the God of the Old Testament, is the one who holds the earth in the hollow of his hand, who sits enthroned above all the rulers of the world, who controls the heaven of heavens. He is incomparable. For which very good reason there is no sense at all in trusting any other gods. Verses 18-20 compare Israel's powerful God with the so-called gods of the heathen, whether the heathen are rich (in which case they make gold and silver gods) or poor (in which case wood has to do instead). The contrast is painfully acute. We look around us at the world, and at the kingdoms of the world, and see that God made them all and rules them all. Then we look down for a moment to the shadows of the earth, and there, of all things, are people trying to *make* their own gods. It is ridiculous but true.

Sadly, it is just as true today. Not so often, admittedly, in the same way—we do not usually make little statuettes of gold and silver and then worship them. But idolatry knows no cultural or temporal barriers. We have four-wheeled idols whose worshipers spend all their effort and money polishing them and driving them faster and faster. We have three-bedroomed idols, whose devotees have to keep them spotlessly clean in case visitors should come. We have square idols with

silver screens. Some of us have well-bound idols with pages
and dust jackets. And like all idols, we worship them because
we get pride out of them. We put ourselves into them, in fact
or in imagination, and then worship what we see. There was a
book written some years ago with the title *The God I Want*. If
ever there were a recipe for idolatry, that is it. The God of the
Bible is not necessarily the God I want: my confused desires
almost certainly don't fit in with who he actually is, and just as
well. What matters much more is the God who actually made
me, the God with whom (whether I want to or not) I have to
do business. And he is so much bigger and greater than anything that I could imagine that I must never imagine I have got
him tied down and pigeonholed. We need to be constantly
looking harder at the God of the Bible. Otherwise we shall
discover that gradually the picture we have of him gets domes-
ticated, whittled down to something we can live with. And
gods that we live with comfortably are idols.

Here in Isaiah, then, we see the true God and the false
gods—the living God and the dead gods—the speaking God
and the dumb gods—the almighty God and the powerless,
man-made imitation idols. We cannot avoid the question:
Which one is it that we worship?

Nor is this just a matter of getting the right answer to a
problem for the sake of academic accuracy. It is a severely
practical matter. The prophet was writing to people who felt
let down by their God—who felt that the threatened exile
meant that Yahweh had forgotten them or was powerless to
help them when they most needed him. The truth was exactly

the opposite. It was they who had forgotten what their God was like. Their God was too small—which was why Isaiah gave them the tremendous vision of God as the Creator and ruler of heaven and earth. Because this God is not only the sovereign ruler: he is the God who shares his own character with his people.

Here we are back where we started, showing just why it is that those who wait on the Lord will renew their strength. *He* does not grow faint (v. 28); *he* gives power to the faint (v. 29); *he* does not grow weary (v. 28 again); those who are weary and exhausted can renew their strength by drawing it from *him* (vv. 29-31). God shares his own self, his almighty power, with those who wait on him. Faith by itself is no good—especially if it is faith in a god who is as powerless as a block of wood! What matters is the Creator God, who is the object of faith.

We could expand this picture to show that other attributes of God's character are there to come to our aid as we need them. When we are up against despair, we must wait upon the God of all love and mercy; when we look death in the face, we must remember that our God is the God who raised Jesus from the dead. The life of the Christian is not something that stands by itself or that props itself up with its own faith. At every point it is based on the character of God, on what God is like. And the climax of the chapter speaks, as has often been pointed out, to the ordinary Christian in everyday life. Mounting up with wings like eagles is all very well. It is often easier to keep going when we are doing something exciting. When life is just the same old thing over and over again, one foot in front of the other, the steady walk without sudden turnings or interests—then it is not always so easy. That is when we need to know about the God who never faints. We sing, at funerals and New Year services, "Time, like an ever-rolling stream, bears all its sons away"—and that is a truth worth pondering in this age when death is the great unmentionable. But beside it we must set, as the hymn does, the truth that God, like an ever-steadfast rock, bears all *his* sons and daughters to glory. His providence undergirds our perseverance.

At this point I want to bring in a passage from Colossians 1, in the RSV in which the apostle Paul neatly picks up and amplifies what Isaiah is saying here. In verse 11 he writes, "May you be strengthened with all power, according to his glorious might, for all endurance and patience with joy." Paul makes no bones about it: being a Christian is a hard business, and requires continual work and vigilance. But this is no cause for despair; he talks of longsuffering *with joyfulness*, because this is God's way of making us saints. In the previous phrase we see the secret: strengthened with all might, he says, according to his glorious power. Not according to how we feel or according to whether we are happy doing the particular task assigned to us for the moment. The word for "according to" in the original Greek is the word we would use for something going down stream—*according to* the current of the river. The current carries the swimmer along with it. He or she has to swim too, of course, but with the help of the current the swimmer can go further and faster, and with less effort, than by his or her own power. And so it is when our weakness swims in the stream of

God's almighty power. Our God is the God who gives power to the faint.

Which brings me back to the beginning again. Faith is not a general trust in something-or-other or someone-or-other; it is looking at our situation and our own frailty in the light of who God is and what he has done for us. Hope, in the same way, is not a vague optimism: it is looking at the future in the light of the same God and what he has promised to do for us, working his purpose out as year succeeds to year. This is a faith and a hope that can go out to "walk worthy of the Lord" (Colossians 1:10 kjv). Without on the one hand any suggestion that God is going to "do it all for us" so that we can sit back and let him get on with it, or on the other hand any idolatrous imagination that our God is not well able to look after us and give us the strength we need as we work for him. When we look at the true God, and wait on him, we find that, when there is mounting up to be done, we can do it with eagles' wings; when there is running to be done, we can do it without weariness; and when there is walking to be done, we can do it—worthy of the Lord—without fainting.

3

NOT BY SIGHT

WE CAN NOW MOVE ON TO LOOK at one of the central passages in the whole Bible dealing with faith. This is Hebrews 11, where the writer says, "Without faith it is impossible to please God" (v. 6).

At once, if we're not careful, we will conjure up in our minds a picture of God as a sort of heavenly examiner who has decided, quite arbitrarily, that he is going to set just one standard as his criterion of passing or failing. Anyone who has faith passes; anyone who does not fails. And not only does that seem arbitrary; if we take the popular view of faith as the next best thing to sheer gullibility, it is decidedly unfair. Why should some people have preferential treatment just because they happen to be capable of swallowing whole certain ideas which other people, perhaps the majority, simply cannot take at any price?

Now it will not surprise you, in view of what has been said already, that I am going to oppose these ideas. I shall let the writer of Hebrews speak in his own defense.

The first thing to notice is directed especially at those who might have the idea that faith is a total certainty about the meaning of life, a complete and clear knowledge of God that enables the person of faith to march calmly through life without batting an eyelid at all the problems and difficulties most of us face. People who think that real faith is like that (whether they are Christians or not) usually end up either in gross self-deception or in wondering why they seem to find faith so difficult. To all this the writer to the Hebrews says plainly: no, you've got it wrong. *Faith is the opposite of sight.* "Faith is the substance of things *hoped for,* the evidence of things *not seen*" (Hebrews 11:1 KJV). Which is why, of course, the title of this chapter is what it is, with a reference to 2 Corinthians 5:7. Faith is not the mysterious ability to sail through life with a secret key that unlocks all the doors. Faith is the willingness to think and act on the basis of what we know of God (which may be very little) and to trust him that he will not let us down. This is equally applicable to people who have believed in God for years but who need faith to see them through the next day, and to people who have never really been sure whether they believed in God or not and therefore need truly to have that faith for the first time.

The writer of Hebrews 11 gives us illustrations of what he means. God says, "Noah, there's a flood coming: go and build an ark"—and Noah, presumably enduring the scorn of the local weather prophets, goes ahead and builds it. God says,

"Abraham, I want you to leave the place where you've been born and bred, and to head off somewhere else; never mind where for the moment. I've got plans for you." Abraham abandons his security and walks by faith, not sight, to the land God was going to give to his descendants. God says, "Sarah, you are going to have a son." In human terms it was impossible. And yet Sarah, behind the nervous and uncertain giggle that Genesis records, believes it, and Isaac is born.

In each case the people concerned are not sort of supermystics who live on a different plane from the rest of us. They are not granted a heavenly map of world events to come. They are given bare promises—that if they go up this particular cul-de-sac God will open before them a door which they could never have dreamed of. This is so today for the Christians who feel that God is calling them to some new path or is instructing them to cut out of their life some treasured possession or relationship or habit. God appears to be saying, "Be a fool. Go out into the wilderness, away from your present secure existence and the things you are leaning on." And in a sense, of course, he is. But those who take him at his word know that it doesn't work out like that. "God has prepared wonderful things for those who love him"—but, as the same passage says, "no eye has seen, nor ear heard, nor the human heart conceived" just what those things are (1 Corinthians 2:9). This is also true for the person who is feeling that to be told "what you need is to believe in Jesus Christ" makes about as much sense as to be told "what you need is an ark." Faith is the opposite of sight. In Proverbs 3:5 we read:

Trust in the LORD with all your heart,
    and do not rely on your own insight.
In all your ways acknowledge him,
    and he will make straight your paths.

Very well, then, faith is not a magic passport to a comfortable, trouble-free life. It is not something reserved for those
who believe in God in the way some people believe the earth
is flat. But there are some who grasp this point almost too
well and go on in consequence to make a virtue out of almost
total agnosticism. There is around today a sort of false humility in matters of faith, which prides itself on the number of
things it isn't quite sure of and walks about in a fog, telling
itself and everyone else that nobody sees these things very
clearly anyway. We sometimes meet it in the form of the person who says, "I can't be doing with all this theologizing,"
when he or she *means*, "If you don't mind, I'd rather not think
too clearly about God and what demands he might be going to
make of me." But that is not faith.

If faith is the opposite of *sight*, it is also the opposite of *doubt*.
Faith is the assurance of things *not seen:* but it is the *assurance* of
things not seen. Beck's American Translation puts it: "Faith is
being sure of the things we hope for, being certain of the
things we do not see." There is, of course, all the room you
like for honest doubt about things we cannot yet know. Abraham didn't know where he was going to end up. But by his
obedience he showed that he was utterly confident that God
would be true to his word. As the writer says a few verses
later, these people died in faith, not having yet received the

promises but having seen them at a distance, and being persuaded of them, and having embraced them. People who live by faith may not know where they are going. They do nonetheless have certainty—certainty in the God who called them and leads them.

If we are going to understand how faith can be the opposite both of sight and doubt, we must stop talking about faith in the abstract and start being more specific. Faith, you see, isn't something useful or valuable in itself. Faith, as we were thinking in chapter two, is like a window, which exists not for its own sake but so that we can see something through it—and so that we can let light into the room. Faith is meaningless and useless unless it looks out on something specific.

The word *something*, however, is misleading. Faith is not a question of abstract theories or of screwing oneself up (as Alice's Queen said) to believe six impossible things before breakfast. Christian faith is not merely giving mental assent to a set of propositions, though it will sooner or later include that. Nor does it mean that any object will do as long as there is faith. Faith means totally relying on God and committing ourselves to God for time and for eternity, trusting his promises, obeying his commands, not trying to make ourselves good enough for him but trusting in the fact that he accepts us as we are because of the work of Jesus Christ on our behalf. Paul, writing from prison, sums it up. "I am," he says, "appointed a preacher, and an apostle, and a teacher . . . [for] which cause I also suffer these things [faith is opposed to sight]: nevertheless I am not ashamed [faith is opposed to doubt]: for

I know whom I have believed [faith is defined by its content], and am persuaded that he is able to keep that which I have committed unto him against that day" (2 Timothy 1:11-12 KJV). I know *whom* I have believed. Faith may sometimes seem like a leap in the dark: but it is always a leap made in obedience to a voice coming out of the darkness which says, "Jump, I'll catch you."

So Christian faith is not a vague optimism or a general religious approach to life. It is believing and trusting in the God who made us and who has shown what he is like in Jesus of Nazareth. And what does that mean? First, it means that we know that God is a holy and almighty God: the life of Jesus leaves us no room for doubt about that. Second, it means he is a loving and merciful God: the death of Jesus leaves us no room for doubt about that. Third, it means he is a God who gives new life: the resurrection of Jesus leaves us no room for doubt about that. We cannot see God: Jesus has shown us what he is like. And what God requires of us is not (in the first instance) great faith. When the disciples said to Jesus, "Lord, increase our faith," Jesus said that all they needed was faith like a grain of mustard seed. It is not great faith we need: it is faith in a great God. Hence the title of this book. And this faith comes, like Abraham's, through hearing the promises of God, believing them and acting on them.

What are these promises, and who are they for? They are for all of us: for those who have been Christians for as long as they can remember, and who need to hear again the life-giving words God speaks; for those who are muddling along as Christians, who need to draw strength for the next days and weeks from the power and love of God; to those who have never yet put their trust in God and who need to do so more urgently than they may think. To all of us the promises come: "He who hears my word," says Jesus, "and believes in him who sent me, has eternal life." Or again: "Come to me, all you that are weary and are carrying heavy burdens, and I will give you rest." Or again: "God so loved the world that he gave his only Son, so that everyone who believes in him may not perish but may have eternal life."

One of the most amazing promises is to be found in this very passage from Hebrews that we have been examining. Having described the faith which is both the opposite of sight and the opposite of doubt, the writer says of these men and women of faith: "Therefore God is not ashamed to be called their God" (Hebrews 11:16). That little possessive adjective, *their* God, sums it all up. God does not want to be remote, and will not be remote, from his people. Christian faith is a relationship—a personal relationship—in which God knows and loves and cares for his people, and in which his people know and love and obey him. That is the promise of God. One might be tempted to say "take it or leave it." But I would like to say "take it."

4

THE BURNING BUSH

ONE OF THE GREAT HEROES OF FAITH in Hebrews 11 is Moses. But Moses crops up earlier in the book as well, in chapter 3, and there he is not just a magnificent example of what God can do in a person of faith. There he is compared to Jesus himself. Not, of course, that Moses comes particularly well out of the comparison. Who would? But to look at Moses for a while in the light of Hebrews 3 will take us neatly from thinking about faith to focusing on Christ, which is faith's constant task. Let's begin at the beginning, back in Exodus.

You remember the story: Moses, with visions of grandeur and dreams of setting his people free, had tried to start a one-man Israelite Liberation Army and quickly found himself obliged to leave Egypt in a hurry. He goes off to the land of Midian, does a good turn for some shepherdesses, gets introduced to their father, comes in for a meal, stays and becomes in turn the husband of one of the daughters, the father of a son and the shepherd of Jethro's sheep. So we find him in Exodus

3 on the mountain, learning how to look after a flock of silly animals in a wilderness. Which, when you think about it, was no bad thing. Because meanwhile, back in Egypt, God heard the groaning of his people Israel and remembered his covenant with Abraham, Isaac and Jacob. And God appeared to Moses to commission him to do with divine power what he had failed to do by himself. As the psalmist says—God led his people like sheep, by the (practiced) hand of Moses and by that of Aaron.

And this commissioning ceremony, which took place in the magnificent scene of the burning bush, consisted principally in a revelation of God's character. Moses is very much a shadowy figure in the whole story. All he does is take off his shoes, hide his face in fear, proclaim his own unworthiness for the task and state his ignorance even of God's name.

All of this is, of course, the right and proper response to the self-revelation of the God who is not inadequately portrayed as a burning fire, as the God of Abraham, Isaac and Jacob, as the God who makes grand promises for the future, and as the God whose very name, insofar as we can begin to understand it at all, proclaims his greatness and eternity. Moses may have gone out into the wilderness as a failed revolutionary. He came back as one who had less confidence in himself than ever, but as one who had met God, and whose boldness in the face of Pharaoh came not from himself but from the God who had promised to be with him.

It is only right that we should begin with the story of Moses, because if we didn't, and moved at once into Hebrews 3, we might very easily forget that when we mention Moses we do not mean a man who did something of some importance way back in the Old Testament and who has little to teach us today. Moses had an experience of God and a knowledge of God which we would do well to envy. In consequence it is said of him that he was the meekest man on earth. We could do with a few more like him today. And it is against this background and no other that we may presume to read Hebrews 3, where it is said that just as the architect is worthy of more honor than the house, so Jesus is worthy of more than Moses.

This is not being patronizing or disparaging about Moses. It simply says that the glory which belongs to Jesus Christ is so supreme, so dazzling, so magnificent, that even Moses is nothing beside it. Even Moses was just a servant in the household; Christ is the son and heir. And this shows us the greatness of Moses, as well as the fact that he must be subordinate to Christ. These two things are perhaps the heart of the matter. The Exodus and the law were great and mighty acts and revelations of God. But they gain their importance not from themselves but from that to which they point. It was at Passover time, Exodus time, that Jesus fed the people in the wilderness with the true bread from heaven. It was at Pentecost, law-giving time, that Jesus, having gone up (like Moses on the mountain), gave to his people the new law of love, written on their hearts by his Spirit.

That takes us at once to John 6, where Jesus echoes again the themes and words of the Exodus. The people—every bit as silly and sheep-like as the Israelites of the Exodus—come with their questions and doubts, and Jesus teaches them. They come hungry, and Jesus feeds them. And, as Moses asked God his name, Jesus reveals his, in one of those great "I am" sayings which come throughout John's Gospel, as clear an indication of who Jesus really was as John could give to his Jewish readers. "I am," says Jesus, "the bread of life. Whoever comes to me will never be hungry, and whoever believes in me will never be thirsty" (John 6:35). In other words, in terms of the Exodus story, Jesus stands in some ways in the place of Moses, but in other and more important ways in the place of God himself. That is why, when we come to take him at his word, to feed on the bread of life, Moses, though only a servant and not the son, is still our example. Like him, we must come with a great sense of our own unworthiness. We must take off the shoes of our pride, and cover the face of our self-centeredness and sin. And we must offer to God not our own plans and splendid abilities (Moses had to give all that up), but our empty hands and hearts, to be filled and indwelt by God himself. And who is this God? None other than the God of the burning bush, the God of Abraham, Isaac and Jacob—the God who reveals himself and gives himself in the Lord Jesus Christ, who has led us out of Egypt and now feeds us as we travel home to the Promised Land.

5

HOLY IS THE LORD

IN CASE THERE'S ANY DOUBT LEFT after thinking about the burning bush, let's move straight to Isaiah 6, where again the message is clear: seeing God is not a comfortable experience.

"Holy, Holy, Holy is the LORD of hosts;
the whole earth is full of his glory." . . .
And I said: "Woe is me! I am lost." (Isaiah 6:3, 5)

Comfortable? Not for Isaiah. We sometimes think, though, that seeing God *ought* to be comfortable. We talk happily about people having a sort of "God-shaped blank" in their lives, as though all we had to do was to slot God into the blank and everything would be all right. Not a bit of it. Remember Isaiah 40? Israel's trouble was exactly this: they started with a God-shaped blank and ended up with a blank-shaped God. And what use is that? The God of the Bible is not a blank; he has very definite characteristics (notice how much easier it is to fit a *vague* God into a blank), and when he comes into what we call our God-shaped blank, he has to stretch it and pull it and work at it all our lives to turn it into *his* shape.

And what is that shape? Of the dozens of ways we can attempt to describe it—none of which, of course, certainly in our dealing with them here, will do more than begin the task—perhaps the central one is the fact that our God is a holy God. In one sense, all that is to be said about God could be summed up in this point, that he is holy, just as all the colors of the spectrum come through the prism into one pure white light. We shall be thinking about one aspect of this in chapter six, namely, the way holiness shows God as a *personal* God over against nature worship or idolatry. But here we are going to look in some detail at Isaiah 6 to see how the revelation of God's pure holiness, which the prophet receives, is then transformed into the many colors of the gospel. There are three main aspects here, and everything else is contained within them.

The first aspect of God's holiness we might simply call God's *majestic holiness*. We can see this in what Isaiah saw and in what he heard. He saw none other than Israel's God himself, veiled by the wings of his attendant angels, just as in John's similar vision in Revelation 4 the figure on the throne is never described in himself. As the old King Uzziah died, the eternal King revealed himself to the prophet. As Uzziah, who had sinned grievously and incurred leprosy as a result, was taken from his people, God showed himself as the constant and holy King, the sovereign Lord of all. The prophet's eyes saw the King in his beauty, wreathed as always in smoke, hailed by the angels—and majestic in his holiness.

The song he heard emphasizes the point. But what does *holy* mean? We think of it as meaning "extremely good," or words to that effect. But its basic meaning in Hebrew is "set apart," removed at a distance from something. But what is the holy God set apart from? No problem—me! And all of us, since we are all in our fallen humanity sinners, set apart from God. He is, says Habakkuk in a famous passage, "of purer eyes than to behold evil" (Habakkuk 1:13 RSV). And when Isaiah hears this song, there is only one response (though it may take different forms). Moses took off his shoes; John and Ezekiel both fell on their faces (Revelation 1; Ezekiel 1). Isaiah expresses the same conclusion in words: "Woe is me!" he says, "I am lost." The vision of God's majestic holiness reveals to the prophet, inescapably, his own utter unworthiness. And this leads at once into the second point to be seen in this passage.

The second and inevitable aspect of this revelation is what we may call God's *judgment holiness*. God's holiness shows up sin as a clear light must show up the dark corners of a room. And the sin it reveals is sin in both the man of God, Isaiah, and the people of God. Isaiah himself says: "Woe is me! I am lost, for I am a man of unclean lips." Why lips? Well, for a start Isaiah has just listened to the heavenly choirs praising God with sinless voices—and the contrast with his own use of his vocal organs must have been painful. But Isaiah is aware in addition of the truth which Jesus pointed out so graphically, that what the mouth says shows what the heart is full of. If the lips are unclean, it is because the heart is too. God's judgment holiness pierces through our half-hearted worship with the revelation of what pure worship would be like and challenges our sinful hearts with the vision of beings whose hearts and lips are totally in tune with the will of God. If we applied the first to our church services and prayer meetings, and the second to our everyday speech, we would be a lot better for it.

Isaiah, the man of God, however, although confronted as an individual, is very much aware of deeper dimensions to sin than just his personal uncleanness. He dwells, he says, in the midst of a people of unclean lips, and that is just the symptom, the outward sign of a people whose whole life was slanted away from taking God seriously. We can see how this worked out if we turn back a page or two, to the stinging accusations Isaiah flung at his contemporaries. Chapters 1–5 are full of God's judgment holiness. (This part of the book may have been put together as an introduction to the rest of the prophet's message, and particularly to provide us with the necessary dark backdrop to the story of his call.)

Chapter 1 denounces the people for infidelity to Yahweh. The people "have despised the Holy One of Israel," and in consequence their worship is nothing but sham ritual. And where God is despised and worship hollow, the soil is ripe for every kind of social injustice (v. 23). Chapter 2, after its opening vision of the restored Zion, continues with the warning of terrible judgment on those who combine idol worship with commercialism. And chapter 3 threatens that God will allow the nation that Israel has become to fall into corrupt and ineffectual government. The dreary progress of sin is set out for all to see: the people have spoken against the Lord, "defying his glorious presence" (v. 8), they have twisted justice, preyed on the poor and denied them their rights, and lived in arrogant luxury (vv. 9, 14-23).

Then, after the renewed promise of chapter 4, the indictment is given the extra note of personal sorrow with the song in chapter 5 of the vineyard that produced wild grapes. What are these wild grapes? Again we get the catalog: grandiose property development which takes no thought of the poor, drunken orgies and, in and through it all, persistent and willful arrogance toward God. To read Isaiah 5:19 and following produces a very clear impression of the typical Israelite of Isaiah's day. This is how they talk and think: "You say Yahweh is a sovereign God, who is holy and powerful—well, sorry, but that's not the sort of God we want. We want a nice meek God who'll do what we want and give us all the fun we want . . . don't talk to us about strict moral standards—strict morals are the real evil, and the real good is doing what you like [v. 20] . . . all right, let God go on being holy and sovereign if he wants to—why not get him to do something positive so that we can see what you mean [v. 19] . . . just let us get on with our pleasures—a few people may get hurt, so what? It's every man for himself in this world, you know [vv. 22-23]."

What does God have to say about a people who talk like that? He declares through his prophet that when his people show such carelessness about him and consequently such callousness toward one another (especially for the weak members of the community), then they are ripe for judgment. God's judgment holiness is revealed not only against sin in the man of God but also against sin in the people of God. And this judgment begins with a process of hardening, designed to fit Israel all the quicker for the judgment which is to come upon them. Here we are back in Isaiah 6 again.

We find something curious at this point. When Isaiah 6 is read in church, the reader is usually instructed to stop at verse 8. This makes a nice little point to round off a nice little sermon—forgiveness (v. 7) leading to God's call (v. 8) heard and obeyed. All very challenging. But in our individualistic presentations of the gospel—not to mention our dislike for anything that seems to be too harsh in our view of God—we shut off Isaiah just as he is getting to the point where the first five chapters have been leading. God does not leave the prophet without a message to proclaim. And what a message!

> Go, and say to this people:
> "Keep listening, but do not comprehend;
> Keep looking, but do not understand."
> Make the mind of this people dull,
>   and stop their ears,
>   and shut their eyes,
> so that they may not look with their eyes,
>   and listen with their ears,
> and comprehend with their minds,
>   and turn and be healed.
> Then I said, "How long, O Lord?" And he said:
> "Until cities lie waste

without inhabitant,
and houses without people,
and the land is utterly desolate;
until the LORD sends everyone far away,
and vast is the emptiness in the midst of the land.
Even if a tenth part remain in it,
it will be burned again,
like a terebinth or an oak
whose stump remains standing
when it is felled."
The holy seed is its stump. (Isaiah 6:9-13)

A strange, terrible, beautiful passage. Yet—can this be the God we know? Is our God-shaped blank big enough to take *this?* The answer is simple. If it isn't, it won't take Jesus either. These verses—or rather the first half of them, the most terrible part—are found on Jesus' lips in Matthew, Mark and Luke. John uses them to describe Jesus' ministry and its effects, and Paul uses them (in Acts, and refers to a similar point in Romans) to describe the effects of his own ministry. It is clear that we have here a statement of God's constant attitude toward his people when they are sunk in sin. We see just the same thing over and over again in Old and New Testaments alike, but we needn't move out of Isaiah for another example. In Isaiah 42:24-25 the prophet says:

Who gave up Jacob to the spoiler,
and Israel to the robbers?
Was it not the LORD, against whom we have sinned,

in whose ways they would not walk,
   and whose law they would not obey?
So he poured upon him the heat of his anger
   and the fury of war;
it set him on fire all around, but he did not understand;
   it burned him, but he did not take it to heart.

There is no escaping it. When the truth dawns about God the King, about the kingdom of God (that is the context of the passages in the Synoptic Gospels and Acts in which the quotations come), its effect is that it actually hardens whose who are ripe for judgment.

What does this mean—what could it possibly mean—for us today? Cities without inhabitants—houses without people? This is, remember, not just the Lord judging a nation: this is God's judgment holiness revealed against his own people—his church. Can it be that God would do this to his people again?

It has happened before. Where are the churches in Ephesus and Colosse? Where is the amazing church in Antioch? Where is the church in Egypt, which stood firm for the truth under Athanasius? Or the church in North Africa, which flourished under Cyprian and Augustine? Why should it be so difficult to imagine that one day historians should ask: Where is the church in England, or America, or anywhere else? Or, where are the Christians who contend for the truth today? We have full churches, strong Christian organizations, thriving colleges, famous preachers. Surely, we say, God wouldn't take all this away? Surely this is God's work—surely he won't destroy what he has built up so carefully?

What do you think all Jerusalem was saying to Isaiah? After all, what did the people have? They had the temple—the place where God had promised to meet with his people. They had the king in the line of David, whom God had said he would treat as his own son. They had Jerusalem itself—the city in which God had chosen to put his name, the city he had sworn to defend. And what was God now saying to Israel? "I will tear down your precious temple; I will send your rebellious king into captivity; and I will reduce Jerusalem to a heap of rubble. And (for good measure) if anyone manages to salvage something out of the wreckage, I shall burn it up again—if there is so much as a stump left of the tree, I shall set it on fire again until it is just a charred blot on the landscape." Jerusalem had forgotten what God was like. They laughed at his holiness and scoffed at his sovereignty. If we don't want to weep for our Christian organizations, for our churches, for our colleges and seminaries, then the remedy is clear.

But if we leave the picture there, we have only half the message. We have seen God's majestic holiness, revealed in angelic glory; we have seen his judgment holiness, revealed against his sinning people. We must now look at the third aspect of God's revelation of holiness, what we might call his *gospel holiness*. In wrath, God remembers mercy.

There is a standard mistake we must avoid at this point. When we think of God being angry and then think of him being merciful, it is all too easy to imagine that God takes off one mask and puts on another one, as though he suddenly changed his mind and decided not to be angry after all. Not

so. For a start, as we shall see, God's mercy as well as his judgment grows out of his holiness. Once we see holiness, we see
judgment and mercy together.

This is clear in a passage like Isaiah 48:9-11. There God
declares that the reason he will save his people is the same as
the reason he will judge them, namely, for the sake of his name
and his holiness, for the sake of his own glory. God is no fairy
godmother, coming to wave a magic wand and make everything all right after all. The sovereign God of Israel is a God
who loves his people with a holy love, because of which, in
great kindness, he so acts to bring glory to his name that he
also brings salvation, joy, peace and happiness to his chosen
people.

In any case, God's mercy is not something totally apart
from his judgment. On the contrary, the mercy grows out of
the judgment. God's mercy consists (at least partly) in this,
that he uses the judgment that must fall on sin as the means by
which he brings mercy to his people. Once again Isaiah has to
experience in himself the message which he is to preach.

What do you think went through Isaiah's mind when he saw
this awesome figure coming toward him with a burning coal,
making as if to touch his lips with it—those lips which, you
remember, Isaiah had just recognized were sinful? The effect
is quite different from the burning judgment Isaiah no doubt
expected. When the coal touches his lips, it is accompanied by
a word of mercy: the fire has not burned him but has rather
purged away his sin. Isaiah needed to learn this lesson. It is
exactly the point God wanted him to preach. As so often,

when God wants to give a message to a preacher, he first burns that message into the person, so that he or she will speak from the heart.

So now we can look at the other half of the picture—God's gospel holiness applied to Israel. As there is mercy for the man of God (Isaiah), so there is mercy for the people of God. But it too grows out of judgment. We see it in Isaiah 6:13, at the end of the verse. Although some modern translations have followed the Greek version of the Old Testament and have left out the relevant words, they are there in the oldest Hebrew manuscripts and should certainly be kept. In the New Revised Standard Version the verse runs:

"And if a tenth part remain in it,
    it will be burned again,
like a terebinth or an oak
    whose stump remains standing
    when it is felled."
The holy seed is its stump.

Now what can all this be about?

The illustration is clear, once we work it out. The picture Isaiah is drawing for us is of a tree being felled, and then the stump being burned so that all we can see is a charred mess where once there was a tree. But sometimes that is the only way to save a tree. Save it? Yes. It may not look like it, but there is still life in the stump, and next year or the year after there will be new shoots coming out of that charred mess, new life where all that could be seen was death. But what is this new life? Isaiah calls it the "holy seed," the stump which looks dead but is not. In the context of the chapter this must mean that the seed is life from the Holy One himself, divine life, waiting until Israel has been purged of its sin before it will burst forth in new glory.

We can see the picture more clearly if it is thrown onto a bigger screen, and this is what Isaiah proceeds to do. (For those who may be interested, there are several worthwhile Bible studies waiting to be done on the use of the "seed" idea throughout Isaiah.) In the end of Isaiah 10 and the beginning of chapter 11 we see the principle applied, and now there is no mistaking what is going on. Chapter 10 closes with a further terrible warning of God's judgment against his sinful people:

> Look, the Sovereign, the LORD of hosts
>   will lop the boughs with terrifying power;
> the tallest trees will be cut down,
>   and the lofty will be brought low.
> He will hack down the thickets of the forest with an axe,
>   and Lebanon with its majestic trees will fall. (Isaiah
>   10:33-34)

Here is the same picture of judgment we have just seen in Isaiah 6:9-13. The great trees are to come down. But now go on to Isaiah 11:1-2:

> A shoot shall come out from the stump of Jesse,
>   and a branch shall grow out of his roots.
> The Spirit of the LORD shall rest on him.

So the prophet builds up, from the broken-down stump of the condemned nation, the glorious picture of the holy Seed himself, God's promised future King in whose days there will be justice, peace and a world full of the knowledge of the Lord. This is the promise of Isaiah 6:13 with its colors filled in.

We should not miss the implications of this picture. Like many other Old Testament images, it forms an outline, a pattern, whose detail we can fill in from the fuller revelation which we have. This comes out in Jesus' quotation, on the night he was betrayed, of Zechariah 13:7-9, the terrible passage in which God declares that he will "strike the shepherd, that the sheep may be scattered." The passage in Zechariah is very similar to the end of Isaiah 6: God will purify and purge the people until they are truly his. By applying this passage to himself Jesus shows how he understands his own death. He sees himself as the last remnant of Israel, bearing in himself the purging and purifying of the nation. Israel is cut down to one man, and that one man is put to death; and from that point on God begins to restore his people. The resurrection of Jesus is God's new start for his true people.

This is just the process we find in Psalm 126, which again has close links with the end of Isaiah 6.

> Those who go out weeping,
>   bearing the seed for sowing,
> shall come home with shouts of joy,
>   carrying their sheaves. (Psalm 126:6)

Even so, Jesus went on his way, to Gethsemane and to the

cross, with tears over Jerusalem, tears as he bore the sin of the world, tears as God's good seed was sown and placed dead in the earth (John 12:24). The holy Seed bore the promises of God through the grave and out the other side, to rise again and bring with him the sheaves of God's harvest, all those ransomed ones who will return to Zion with singing (Isaiah 35:10). This is where the church finds its true source. This is where its life begins and must continue. The holiness of God is finally revealed in Jesus, whose death and resurrection combine God's majestic holiness, God's judgment holiness and God's gospel holiness. Our worship and life are only genuine insofar as they reflect this total revelation of God.

Worship the Lord in holy splendor:
tremble before him, all the earth. (Psalm 96:9)

6

BREAKFAST BY THE SHORE

ONE OF THE CURIOUS THINGS ABOUT our modern society is that while most people are materialists in practice, many of them are rather partial to a good old pagan festival now and again. We have a splendid one in Oxford. Every year on the first of May hundreds of people gather on Magdalen Bridge very early in the morning, and with music and dancing celebrate the fact that spring has come again. People may confess with their lips that materialism is Lord, but some of them at any rate seem to believe nonetheless that life does come out of death. People who say that what we can touch and see is all there is are faced from time to time with the fact that nature, on a brilliant May morning, points away from itself, or perhaps deep within itself, to the truth we all recognize in such an obvious thing as Shakespeare's "Now is the winter of our discontent made glorious summer." The power of the metaphor comes from the appeal to the universal experience of joy at new life where there seemed to be none. Just think of that tremendous passage in the Song of Solomon:

> Arise, my love, my fair one,
>   and come away;
> for now, the winter is past,
>   the rain is over and gone.
> The flowers appear on the earth;
>   the time of singing has come. (Song of Solomon
>   2:10-12)

Now it is of course no accident that Christians have frequently regarded those words as in some way prophetic of what Christ says to his church, particularly as in his resurrection he comes alive on the other side of death to welcome his people with him into newness of life. But having drawn the parallel between our splendid Oxford pagan spring festival and the resurrection, I must also draw attention to a great difference between them. We believe that once in the past, but with the intention of repeating the performance on a grand scale in the future, God did in the life of a *man* what he has always been doing, in one way or another, in the world. He gave new life where, humanly speaking, there was nothing but death. The myth has come true, not just as a "true myth" (whatever that may be) but as human history.

We then find that, as we think about the meaning of the resurrection, the pagan myth itself, having suffered a death in the events of Easter weekend, is itself brought to life again, not now as an old roguish master but as the servant of the truth. Listen to how John tells what happened on a spring morning beside the sea (John 21). Remember how, in this Gospel light, and dark, night and day are such important themes to express truths about God and Jesus. The disciples, he says, "went out and got into the boat, but that night they caught nothing. Just after daybreak, Jesus stood on the beach . . ."—and we can feel instantly, behind those simple words, the whole weight of the knowledge that the church in the person of Jesus, has come through the night of condemnation and impossibility into a spring morning of joy and hope. Then, of course, the whole scene comes to life. What the disciples had been unable to do without Jesus they can do easily and highly effectively at his bidding. Significantly, perhaps, it is only when they have obeyed his command that the disciples realize who it is that has been addressing them from a hundred yards away on the shore.

This last point gives us an important clue to understand the subtle but all-important distinction between the sense of awe and amazement any healthy pagan can feel on a superb May morning and the awe and amazement in the story John tells— particularly when Jesus says, "Come and have breakfast," and John says that none of the disciples dared ask him who he was, knowing it to be the Lord. What has happened to the pagan awe and wonder is that it has become personal, and in becoming personal it has also become ethical. The beauty and power of John's narrative is the beauty and power of sheer holiness, as we saw it in chapter five: the holiness of a life that has faced sin and death and defeated them both, and has now burst through to a realm where we can say, "The death he died, he died to sin, once for all; but the life he lives, he lives to God"

(Romans 6:10). That is why it is only in the act of obedience—
the only proper response to the revelation of God's holiness in
Jesus—that the disciples recognize him. The beauty of holiness includes within it the beauty of spring, but goes far beyond it. We only have to be up at five on one fine morning in
the year to understand the pagan mystery. You have to share in
the risen life to understand the Christian one.

We are sometimes privileged to glimpse this awe and reverence when we meet a Christian of humble self-effacing holiness (as opposed to the proud sort of holiness that inflicts itself
on all in sight). But we ought also to know it when Christ
commands us to bring our lives and achievements (which
themselves are his miraculous gift) and put them before him,
as the disciples brought their 153 fish to shore. They then
found, incidentally, that though it was impossible for them to
fish without Jesus' help, he could feed them without theirs. As
once before at Passover time (back in John 6) Jesus fed the
people with loaves and fishes and told them that he himself
was the living bread, so that anyone who eats of him has eternal life and will be raised up at the last day—so once again he
feeds the disciples with loaves and fishes, but this time having
already himself defeated death. And he invites his church in
this way, week by week and year by year, to come and feed on
him, rejoicing that the long night of sin and death is over and
that the sun of righteousness is risen. But if the Communion
service is to be a truly Christian mystery, and not to lapse into
a semipagan ritual, we must remember to hold our awe and
reverence firmly in the context of holiness. Those who cele-

brate only a pagan festival (whether in spring or at Christmas or harvest) can enjoy the thrill for the moment and then go off and continue to live as pagans. Those who obey Christ's command to come and have breakfast with him must also, being themselves risen with him, seek the things that are above.

7

TO DIE FOR THE PEOPLE

SOMETIMES IT HAPPENS THAT AN ordinary, matter-of-fact statement takes on a new meaning for someone when they see it in a new light. One person says brightly, "Oh, it's nearly four o'clock," intending nothing more by the remark than, "Let's stop work for a moment and have a cup of tea." But another person may be listening whose thoughts are a long way from tea. He is going for an important interview at 4:30, and is already getting nervous about it. The reminder that the fateful time is coming closer and closer makes him jump, and he gets more nervous still.

Now this sort of double meaning is one of the most interesting features of the way John's Gospel is written. John is forever showing us people who say something about Jesus that they mean in almost a casual way, an off-the-cuff remark which doesn't have much significance for the speaker, but which has behind it a profound truth that John intends us to grasp. A good example is the way Pontius Pilate had a notice

written saying "Jesus of Nazareth, the King of the Jews" and
stuck it up on the cross for everyone to see. Pilate meant it
simply as a snub to the Jewish leaders, and they certainly took
it that way. But John intends us to see behind the callous action to the real truth, that Jesus, just because of the cross, is
indeed the King—not of the Jews only but of the whole
world.

In this chapter we are going to begin with another classic
instance of a double meaning in John and use it as a way in to
examine the significance of the cross. From there we shall go
on to see what this meant for Peter in the same chapter that
we were looking at a moment ago (John 21). We begin with
John 11:47-53.

This shows us a group of worried politicians. Faced with an
uprising within their country, led by a man performing miraculous signs, they are scared stiff that the occupying power
will clamp down on them for allowing such a thing and will
destroy their precious national security and identity. Listen to
what they say (v. 47). The chief priests and Pharisees called a
meeting of the Sanhedrin, and asked, "What are we to do?
This man is performing many signs. If we let him go on like
this, everyone will believe in him, and the Romans will come
and destroy both our holy place and our nation." But wily old
Caiaphas knows a trick or two. He is a hard-bitten, hard-faced
religious politician if ever there was one. We might call him
"the unacceptable face of Pharisaism." "Come on!" he says.
"No use talking like that. Don't you see—if he dies, then the
whole nation will be let off! What are you worrying about?

Let the Romans kill this man Jesus: much better than killing all of us." Here is the voice of the cynical schemer, prepared to bargain with other's lives.

Yes, says John in commenting on this: but here is also the voice of God. The Jews believed, rightly, that the high priest was God's representative to their nation. Even when the high priest in question was an irreligious and cynical politician like Caiaphas, this didn't stop God from keeping his side of the bargain. If Caiaphas had been a godly man, he would have spoken God's word gladly and willingly. As he is an ungodly man, he speaks it without even realizing what he is saying.

What is he saying? What is this word from God that he speaks? John says (v. 51) that Caiaphas prophesied that Jesus would die for the Jewish nation—and not only for that nation but also for the scattered children of God, to bring them together into one family. (We can see the same sequence of thought in John 10:14-16.) Here is the double meaning we have been coming to. With the benefit of hindsight we can read verse 50 in a different light. "It is better for you to have one man die for the people than to have the whole nation destroyed." Forget for a moment the cynicism of the speaker. What God meant by the statement was something like this. Here is a worldwide people, deserving to die for their sin, scattered and divided by the selfishness and bitterness within human nature. Into this situation God sends Jesus. He is to die, so that his people need not. One man dies, and the people go free. Jesus represents in himself the whole people of God, Jew and Gentile alike. His death is counted by God in place of theirs.

To look at it another way, on the cross Jesus was to establish once and for all the church, the true people of God. The Jewish politicians were worried about their nation and its future. God's answer to them is that by Jesus' death he will lay the foundations of a new people, a worldwide people. Jesus, God says through Caiaphas, will die not only for the nation but also to bring together the scattered children of God from all over the world. We could sum up this passage as "the confession of the cynic." If we ask the question, as many do, "Why the cross?" the answer given here is that Jesus was to die so that his people, the true children of God, should not die. The confession of the cynic shows us the purpose of God to save his people.

We must now move on, from the confession of the cynic, to the crucifixion of the Savior. The story of Jesus' death is well known, but its meaning is not always understood. A good deal of what John intends us to understand by it is focused in three verses from chapter 19:

> After this, when Jesus knew that all was now finished, he said (in order to fulfill the scripture), "I am thirsty." A jar full of sour wine was standing there. So they put a sponge full of the wine on a branch of hyssop and held it to his mouth. When Jesus had received the wine, he said, "It is finished." Then he bowed his head and gave up his spirit. (John 19:28-30)

Which "scripture" did Jesus fulfill? John clearly intends that we should think of Psalm 69, which is written out of an experience of great suffering, and shows how God uses that suffer-

ing as a means to the end of saving his people. In the middle of
that psalm we read:

> Insults have broken my heart,
>> so that I am in despair.
> I looked for pity, but there was none;
>> and for comforters, but I found none.
> They gave me poison for food,
>> and for my thirst they gave me vinegar to drink.
> (Psalm 69:20-21)

In his thirst, and in the drinking of the vinegar, Jesus con-
sciously accepts the role, set out in the Old Testament, of the
one who was to suffer so that God's salvation could come upon
his people. This ties in exactly with what Caiaphas said. Jesus
dies so that the people may not die.

Jesus' thirst also points to a theme John uses a good deal in
the Gospel. In chapter 4 Jesus tells the woman of Samaria that
he can give her a drink from the water of life, which will satisfy
her spiritual thirst once and for all. In chapter 7 he says, "Let
anyone who is thirsty come to me, and let the one who believes
in me drink. As the scripture has said, 'Out of the believer's
heart shall flow rivers of living water'" (John 7:37-38). John
makes it clear as he records these sayings that the water of life is
a vivid way of describing the life of God himself, which Jesus is
offering to all. Humanity's deepest need—its deepest longing—is for fellowship with God. Humans need and long to
know God in an intimate and personal relationship, and again
and again Jesus describes this longing as a great *thirst* for the

water of life. And now Jesus himself is hanging on a cross, saying, "I am thirsty."

They gave him not water, but *vinegar* to drink. Sour wine wets the tongue, but it does not quench the thirst. For the first time in his life, Jesus himself knew what it was to be cut off from the presence of God, from the source of true living water. On the cross he took on himself that separation from God which all others know. He did not deserve it: he had done nothing to warrant being cut off from God, but as he identified himself totally with sinful humanity, the punishment that sinful humanity deserved was laid squarely on his shoulders. Caiaphas said that Jesus would die so that his people would not die. Jesus achieved this by suffering not only physical death but spiritual death, accepting for himself what all but he deserved. That is why he shrank, in Gethsemane, from drinking the "cup" offered to him: he knew it to be the cup of God's wrath. On the cross Jesus drank that cup to the dregs, so that his sinful people might not drink it.

He drank it to the dregs. He finished it, finished the bitter cup both physically and spiritually. And that turned his last cry into a shout of triumph: It is finished! That is no defeatist, despairing wail. Nor is it the feeling, "Well, at least it's over at last," such as someone might have on getting out of the dentist's chair. It is the word (one word in the original) that would be written on a bill when it had been paid, like a rubber stamp for a receipt. Here is the bill, and on it the word "Finished"— "Paid in full." The debt is paid. The punishment has been taken. Salvation is accomplished.

We must give this word *finished* its full significance. When Jesus died, he did not leave the job half done. If I go to a shop and buy something for my wife to pick up later, the shop does not make her pay for it as well. Jesus has bought salvation on behalf of his bride, the church (see Ephesians 5:25-27). He has paid the price in full. When we come to God and pray that he will save us, he does not say, "All right, but first you must do this, or that—you must set about making yourself a better person, you must pay some penalty for all you have done wrong to date." When we come to God for salvation, he knows that it is already ours for the asking. The crucifixion of the Savior means that the price has already been paid in full.

We must now rejoin the scene we left in chapter six, with Jesus and the disciples having breakfast by the shore. To understand this part of the story we need first to go back a little, to one of the most tragic incidents in the New Testament.

You will remember that when Jesus was arrested, Simon Peter tagged along at a distance to see what would happen. While Jesus was on trial, Simon Peter was just outside the room, and some of the people there started to question him about Jesus. Suddenly Peter got the wind up. "Jesus?—Don't know who you're talking about." "Ah," they said, "but we saw you with him." "Rubbish," Peter retorted, quite alarmed now. "I don't even know the man." "But you must be one of his crew; your accent gives you away." At this Peter lost his temper. He used words he hadn't used since the old days back in the fishing boat. Three times he denied even knowing Jesus. And at that moment the cock crowed. Jesus turned and looked at Peter through the open door. Peter remembered Jesus' words to him, that before the cock crowed he would deny him three times. It was all too much, and Peter rushed out and wept as though his heart would break.

I suspect most of us can sympathize with Peter. Even people who have been Christians for many years still know what it is to deny their Lord in what they say or do, and still know in consequence the bitterness that results. Others haven't been following Christ for very long—Peter had been at it three years—and may well feel the pull of the old life, the old language, the old world in which Jesus was something of an embarrassment. Some have never even begun to follow him. Like Peter outside the door, they are near enough to see what is going on but determined to stay at a safe distance. So there is something of Peter in us all. If this is so, we might expect that what Jesus had to say to Peter after the lakeside breakfast might be relevant for us as well.

Jesus had risen again. The disciples had seen him, and now he appeared to them again by the Lake of Galilee. We know from Luke's Gospel that after the resurrection Jesus explained to the disciples how all the Scriptures of the Old Testament foretold his death and resurrection. In the light of this and of the way that Jesus' threefold question to Peter appears to echo deliberately Peter's triple denial, we might imagine the conversation going along the following lines.

Jesus looks around at Peter's fishing boat and tackle. Peter has gone back to the old life again, unsure what to do with himself next. Jesus says, "Simon, son of John, when I first met you, you were a fisherman, and I called you to be a fisher of humans. You were very happy then to come with me and work alongside me. Now you are back here again. Do you love me more than these?" Peter is a bit nonplussed and doesn't know where this is leading, but manages to say: "Yes, Lord—you know I love you." "Well," Jesus says, "I have a job for you. Feed my lambs."

Peter doesn't know what to say to this, but Jesus goes on: "And Peter, you remember how you said you would go with me even to death? How even if all the others left me you wouldn't? It didn't work out like that, did it? I heard you that night, as you know. You told them you didn't even know me. Simon, son of John, do you love me?" Peter hangs his head. There is no denying it now. "Yes, Lord," he says, "you know that I love you."

But Jesus isn't finished yet. There is no point in getting someone to see themselves as they really are if you don't show them where to go from there. "Don't you see, Peter," he says. "That's not the end of the story. Peter, the next day they took me outside the city and they crucified me. They watched me die while you hid away somewhere. But don't you see what it means? I was despised and rejected by everybody. I had nothing but darkness and pain and death. But Peter, I bore all your griefs. I carried all your sorrows. I was wounded for your transgressions. I was bruised for your iniquities. Upon me was the punishment that made you whole. As they beat me, you were being healed. You were straying away like a lost sheep, Peter, but God laid on me the punishment for all your sin.

Simon, son of John, do you love me?"

Peter, feeling that the tears in his eyes tell the truth anyway, says, "Lord, you know all things. You know that I love you." And Jesus goes on to tell him of the new life he must lead, a life of serving God, a life of suffering and death, a life of following the Master.

The story hardly needs applying further. Christian faith begins (or it may begin) with understanding what Peter understood that morning. It is as we see Jesus, dying so that his people need not die, completing on the cross the work of our salvation, wounded for our transgressions and bruised for our iniquities, that we see clearly the love that God has for us. It is also the point at which we begin to love God in return.

8

GOD'S FOOLISH GOSPEL

"ALL THE REALLY SENSIBLE PEOPLE want to see tangible evidence. All the really clever people say they won't believe it until they get a clearly argued case. All I have to offer them is a couple of pieces of wood, a handful of nails, and a broken human body." With three brilliant strokes of his brush, Paul paints for us in 1 Corinthians 1:22-23 the total impossibility of preaching the gospel of the cross we have just been looking at. Jews demand signs; Greeks seek wisdom; we preach Christ crucified. What they want, we haven't got. What we have got, they don't want. Hopeless. And yet hopelessness is, in the wisdom and power of God, the only place hope can start.

The gospel (as everyone knows who believes it and then tries to explain it to a skeptic) is not a straightforward thing. If we bring our human categories of understanding to it and try to fit it into them, it proceeds to shatter them one after the other until there is only one vessel left that can contain it. That vessel is the life of the people of God, and within that people

the life and heart of the person who is indwelt by the Spirit of
God. The gospel was too precious to be cheapened by a sign
that would please the Jews, and too lofty to be forced into
Greek philosophical categories. It is too rich, in the same way,
for the models of thought set up by the psychologist or sociolo-
gist, valuable though they may be in other ways. The gospel is
like nothing else on earth, for the very good reason that it is
like God.

We saw a few chapters ago that it is no good beginning with
a blank-shaped God. The God of the Bible refuses to be fitted
into our blanks: we have to reshape our lives around him. It is
just the same with his gospel, the gospel of the cross of Jesus
Christ. All other religious systems tell humans how to im-
prove themselves, to better their own position by moral effort, to seek their own salvation in greater personal piety or
detachment from the world. God's gospel stands all that on its
head. Human wisdom is simply not the sort of thing required.
It is the person who loses his or her life who will save it. The
person who finds the truth is the one who looks at the crucified Messiah—a contradiction in terms for the Jew, a corpse
on a gallows to the pagan—and who sees there God's way of
salvation, God's way of putting us on the road to life.

The gospel is not, then, the sort of thing that automatically
appeals to human beings as they are in themselves. We speak,
says Paul in the same passage, the wisdom of God in a mystery.
God reveals it to us by his Spirit. When a doctor does a test for
colorblindness, he has a card on which the colorblind person
sees one pattern while the person with normal sight sees an-

other. The gospel of God is like that. We speak the wisdom of God in a mystery, even the hidden wisdom, that God ordained before the world for our glory. No credit to us: left to ourselves we would have seen quite a different pattern in the events of Good Friday. God needs to perform a miracle in our understanding, opening our eyes to see properly for the first time, to realize that the young Jew on the cross is God's salvation for the world. To change the picture, what before looked like a worthless pebble suddenly appears as the pearl of great price. The gospel is a mystery that God alone can reveal.

Knowing that the gospel is a mystery saves us from two opposite dangers as we try to tell people about it. On the one hand, there is no reason to think that people will come to believe in Jesus simply because of our clever arguments. Not that we must not think hard about our faith and give our hearers the fruit of our deepest understanding. Far from it. Nor must we fail to enter into careful and sympathetic discussion and debate with those who do not believe. People often have intricate and well-thought-out reasons for not believing, and we treat them with less than respect if we ignore this. But if a person is to hear the gospel and believe it, the work must be God's, not ours. Paul says that his speech and preaching were not with the enticing words of human wisdom, but in demonstration of the Spirit and power, so that our faith should not rest on human wisdom but on the power of God (1 Corinthians 2:4). We must not encourage others to build on the shifting sand of our limited understanding.

On the other hand, to adapt Jesus' parable in Mark 4, there

is no reason to be afraid that the gospel seed will all fall on stony ground, or be eaten up by the birds of the air, or be choked by weeds. God in his grace will see to it that some will fall on good ground and bring forth fruit. We can therefore have true Christian confidence as we go out to proclaim the good news, since neither the faith we seek to elicit nor the faith with which we go to the task rests in our own wisdom. All is of the power of God and that alone. And God has established it as a principle that his power should be hidden within the gospel of the crucified and risen Jesus.

That is why the statement that evangelism is basically God's work and not ours does not remove the motive to preach the gospel. It sets it on its proper footing. God is not impotent, waiting for us to stir our stumps before he makes a move. He is the omnipotent God (remember Isaiah 40) who has promised to save men and women through the preaching of the gospel. We go to it with confidence, knowing that this is God's appointed way of drawing people to himself. This means, as well, that we dare not water down the gospel to make it fit what people expect, to make it acceptable to modern people. If Paul had been working on that principle, he could never have written 1 Corinthians 1–2. Nor could he have expected that his gospel would do anyone any good. It may be strong medicine when taken, but it is the only medicine with which God has promised to heal us.

The mystery of the gospel, and the mystery of its effect on people, is matched by the mystery that exists within the preacher. I was with you, says Paul, in weakness and in fear and in much trembling. It is when we are weak that we become strong, for in our weakness we learn the futility of all our human effort and see instead the mighty power of God, in whom we trust. We ourselves become like the seed sown (back in Mark 4 again). Our life is hidden with Christ, disappearing from view as we give ourselves completely to him and then miraculously rising up again, like the new corn, into fresh life. We have to go on learning for ourselves the pattern of trusting God to take a situation that looks hopeless in human terms and transform it into the fulfillment of his purposes. This is to walk by faith, not by sight. As we saw earlier in Proverbs 3:5-6:

> Trust in the LORD with all your heart,
>   and do not rely on your own insight.
> In all your ways acknowledge him,
>   and he will make straight your paths.

This is where true faith and true wisdom are to be found. We must set God always before our eyes and believe what he says about the gospel, about ourselves and about those to whom we go with his message of Jesus crucified and risen. This, after all, turns out not only to be wisdom but delight. No eye has seen (says Paul in the same passage), no ear has heard, no mind has imagined, what God has prepared for those who love him. It is as we have and continue to exercise faith in our great God and his gospel that we show our love to him and, in loving him, go out into his world to live for him. And that takes us into the next section of this book.

part two

FAITH TO
LIVE AND LOVE

9

CITIZENS OF JERUSALEM

ONE IMPORTANT PART OF THE Christian's faith in the great
God of the Bible is the belief that he is the Creator God. That
means that the world we live in is, as we say, his handiwork.
God is to the world as a carpenter is to a houseful of furniture.
It is all his own work. When he had made it, he looked at it
and was pleased with what he saw. And (though the tenants of
the house seem to have done their best to spoil it) he still has
plans for it, plans that will complete and make perfect what he
then began.

This means that we have to revise the estimate we so often
make of the world, particularly as Christians. One of the many
ways non-Christian thinking soaks into Christians today is
through a twisting of the Christian truth that God will make
new heavens and a new earth (and that therefore as the J. R.
Baxter song says, "This world is not my home, I'm just
a-passing through") into the idea that we needn't bother about
the old world. It doesn't really matter, we think, what we do

with it or in it, whether we achieve anything worthwhile in it. Provided we get to heaven in the end we need not worry too much about the world.

This turns up in an applied form in the way so many people drift through life always hoping that when they get a better job, or when they finish a student course, or when they get married, or when they move house, then things will matter—but at the moment they are just filling in time, keeping going until the real things begin. In this applied form it means that because life is short we make it also boring and pointless. As a Christian heresy, it means that because we are citizens of heaven we need not bother about being citizens of earth as well.

For some reason the biblical writers didn't see it like that. In this chapter we are going to look at two passages, one from the New Testament and one from the Old, in which the idea of citizenship is brought out.

The first is Philippians 3, especially verse 20. Philippi was a Roman colony, founded by citizens of Rome going to live there. To the church in Philippi Paul writes: we are a colony of heaven, and we are waiting for the day when our citizenship there will be ours to enjoy fully. The church is an outpost of the city of God. Those who belong to the church are citizens already, and they look forward to the coming of the King to take them home where they belong, to give them in full the privileges they are already entitled to. That is why earlier in the letter (1:23) Paul says that his desire is to depart and be with Christ, because that is far better than remaining in this life. This side of the picture is rightly at the heart of all Christian worship, not least holy Communion. We lift our hearts to heaven, where our citizenship belongs and where Christ himself is, and we taste here in our colony the food that is eaten in the mother city. And we long, naturally and rightly, for the day when we will be there ourselves.

However, Paul was not yet there himself. Nor does he regard this as a sad fact at which he must shrug his shoulders and say, "Well, one day soon perhaps." Far from it. To remain in the flesh, he says, is more necessary because of what God wants me to do here and now. Though he is away from the mother city, he takes a thoroughly positive attitude toward his absence and sets about putting it to the best possible use. There is the service of God's people; there is the spread of the gospel in the world; there is the major and lifelong task of holiness, of pressing forward to the goal which is Christ himself.

The work that remains for us to do here in exile is the subject of Jeremiah 29:4-14. This is a curious and interesting passage. Here are the Jewish exiles in Babylon, twiddling their thumbs with nothing to do but sit and mope, longing to get back to Jerusalem. Here are the false prophets, saying to them: Don't worry, the Lord will rescue you very soon. You won't be in Babylon very long. Just stick it out a few months—perhaps a year or two at the outside—and then it will be up and off, back home to Jerusalem.

Jeremiah's message is quite different. You are still citizens of Jerusalem, he says, and you (or your children or grandchildren) will be going back there, in seventy years if you must

know. So while you are here—while you are a little exiled
colony, belonging to Jerusalem but living in Babylon—don't
be negative about Babylon. Don't bear a grudge against it. Settle down. Build houses, get married, bring up families. *Seek
the peace of the city where you are.* Pray to God for it: for in its
peace you shall have peace. Here is the paradox of being a
citizen of Jerusalem: because you belong to Jerusalem, you
can settle down and even be of use in Babylon. It isn't your
home; it isn't where you are going to end up at the last; but it
is where God has put you at the moment, and you gain no extra marks (so to speak) for adopting a superior pose, for thinking that because you are citizens of heaven you are a bit too
good to bother about the shoddy old world you unfortunately
live in at the moment.

On the contrary. The world may look shoddy to us, but it is
still God's world, and as God's people the church has a positive, continuing and creative role to play in it. We are to live
as constructive citizens of the world while we are here. We
are to seek its peace, and pray for it. That is why praying for
the world forms such an important part of all Christian worship. Because we are citizens of heaven temporarily resident in
the world, we bring the world with us before God and seek its
peace. This is what Paul is getting at in 1 Timothy 2:1-2. In the
peace of the world, for which we pray and work as Christians
(and of course in the justice and total good order of the world
as well) the church will be able to serve God properly, and the
gospel will be preached freely throughout the world. In its
peace we will have peace.

This is part of the total royal, priestly ministry of the people of God, being God's appointed rulers over creation and bringing the praises of creation to God, as in Revelation 4—5. It is therefore a sign of the new creation God will make when he brings us home to the heavenly Jerusalem at last. Then, with humanity restored to its rightful place under God and over the world, God will create new heavens and a new earth in which righteousness dwells.

The same pattern works out in the details of our everyday life. This place where we are at the moment may not be our home. The work we are doing at the moment may not be the work we are hoping to do for the rest of our lives. The people we meet today may not be our companions much longer. But the place, the work and the people are the setting God has placed us in right now. God cares about the present as well as the future. In fact, he cares about the present *because* he cares about the future—so different from us: we lose interest in the present through thinking too much about the future. Our life here, the work we do today, the people we meet, though temporary, are real and matter to us and to the world. We must pray for the peace of the world and give ourselves gladly, as citizens of heaven, to the tasks God gives us here and now.

10

CHRISTIAN HYPOCRITES?

A FRIEND OF MINE PREACHED A sermon in which he stood a parable on its head. It went something like this.

Two men went up to the temple to pray. The first was a Pharisee, and the second a publican. And the publican stood up and prayed like this: O God, I thank thee that I am not as other men are: two-faced, holier-than-thou, proud, arrogant, self-righteous, or even as this Pharisee. And the Pharisee would not even lift up his eyes to heaven, but beat upon his breast and said: Lord, have mercy on me, a hypocrite.

Hypocrisy has had a bad press. Quite right too. But this means that it is very difficult for us to come to the subject with a clear head. Because we use *hypocrite* as a general term of abuse, we fail to distinguish between different kinds of hypocrisy, some of which are inescapable and necessary for any Christian and are therefore to be lived with and even welcomed. So when people say, as they do, that surely all religious people are hypocrites, we must answer that probably most of

them are. But we need to understand more clearly what
hypocrisy is before we can isolate why Jesus attacked the
Pharisees, and what it was about them that still lives on in the
church today and must be strenuously avoided. One of the key
passages in this subject is Matthew 6 (part of the Sermon on
the Mount), which we shall refer to from time to time.

What is a hypocrite? Literally, the word means an actor, a
person who plays a part. Someone who is outwardly one thing
and inwardly something quite different. When people say, "I
wouldn't go to church—they're all hypocrites in there," what
they probably mean is that we folk who do go to church pro-
fess to be extra holy people, to have a higher moral code than
anybody else does, and yet in real life from Monday to Satur-
day we are in fact no better than the ordinary people who
don't go to church at all. The impression given here is that it is
better to have low standards than to be hypocritical: I'll come
back to that in a moment. What I want to do now is to look at
Matthew 6 and see, before we get any further, just what Jesus
said about hypocrisy. And remember: the point of all this is
not so that we can all indulge in the inverted snobbery of the
publican in the inverted parable, pointing our finger at other
people for their hypocrisy. What we are trying to do is to see
what Jesus is attacking so we can recognize it in ourselves and
get to work to eradicate it. That is quite enough to be going on
with, without setting everyone else right as well.

In Matthew 5:20 Jesus tells us that our righteousness must
exceed that of the scribes and Pharisees. The rest of chapter 5
is aimed in particular at the scribes; Matthew 6:1-18 is aimed

at the Pharisees. (Note that 6:1 should read: "Beware of practicing your righteousness," not "piety" as in the RSV: if we miss that we miss the sequence of thought from 5:20.) In 6:1-18 there are three area of practical righteousness—of religion, if you like—which Jesus mentions. Verses 2-4 deal with giving money, verses 5-6 with prayer and verses 16-18 with fasting, doing without.

These three sections are closely parallel to each other. Verses 7-15, in the middle, are related to the rest, as we shall see, but they make a rather different point. Let's look at the three main sections together and see what was so wrong about these Pharisees. We shall also draw on Matthew 23, where similar things are said.

First, there is nothing wrong with prayer, fasting or almsgiving themselves. Jesus has not a word to say against any of them. Matthew 23:2—the scribes and Pharisees have the standard right because they quite properly look to Moses for it. But *they concentrate only on the outward appearance.* Matthew 6:2—they sound a trumpet when they are going to give money. This was in fact a regular thing, which we hear about from other sources too. No doubt they would say it was necessary so that the poor would know where and when to turn up: but no doubt too they rather enjoyed the moment when everyone came around the corner and there they were getting ready to hand out the small change.

So too in Matthew 6:5—the Pharisees love to pray at the street corners. This probably means that they prayed in public at the fixed times of prayer, when everyone was expected to

stop what they were doing and pray for a few minutes. Twelve
o'clock strikes: drop your work for a moment and say your
prayers. But somehow the Pharisee just happened to have set
off to go shopping at five minutes to twelve, and, lo and behold, when twelve o'clock strikes he just happens to be cross-
ing the main street, and then, well—we can't set a bad example, now can we?

Then in verse 16—they disfigure themselves to show off
the fact that they are fasting. You get the picture. We are walking down the street minding our own business and suddenly,
hello, there's our old friend the Pharisee, looking as if he'd
been pulled through a hedge backward and got a hangover to
boot. What a marvelously religious man! Fancy being prepared to fast like that; he must be really suffering! And the
Pharisee goes on his way with ashes on his head and a well-
earned glow in his heart. Truly, says Jesus, they have their
reward already.

Matthew 23:5-7 sums the picture up. The Pharisees do all
these things to be seen by others: they make their phylacteries
broad and their fringes long, which is more or less like going
round with a big black Bible sticking out of our pocket where
everyone can see it, and they love the place of honor at feasts,
the best seats in church (presumably where everyone can see
them, clergy take note), and special greetings in the marketplace. And over it all stands Matthew 6:1—"*Beware* of practicing your [righteousness] before men in order to be seen by
them, for then you will have no reward from your Father who
is in heaven." At the heart of pharisaic piety is pride, pride that

is greedy for the applause of others. The Pharisees were quite right to fast, quite right to pray, quite right to give away money, but because the inner motive was wrong, all they concentrated on was the outward appearance and so made the whole thing, outward appearance included, a mockery and a misery.

A misery indeed. Because when all that matters to us is the outward appearance, we make more and more petty rules so as to keep our mind off the big but invisible things. Matthew 23:23—they tithe every last leaf in the garden, but they ignore justice, mercy and faith. What's the point? Nobody notices *them.* And with all these petty manmade rules, the poor ordinary chap gets a raw deal. Pharisees bind up heavy burdens, hard to bear and put them on others' shoulders. They cross land and sea to make one proselyte—one convert to their miserable legalism—and he becomes twice as much a child of hell as they are. They are like people with odd washing-up habits (v. 25): they wash the outside of the cup, so that it looks fine when it's sitting on the shelf, but we're in for a nasty shock if we try to drink out of it.

So we could go on. This is the anatomy of hypocrisy, the hypocrisy Jesus is attacking. Its motive is pride; its method is outward show; its message is self-righteousness. Its results are the hollow praise of others; the overturning of God's true standards of righteousness; the deceit of those who look on, and the judgment of God. May God save us from this hypocrisy.

But how will he save us from it if we are not aware that we are practicing it ourselves? We don't blow trumpets before putting money in the collection. We don't pray in the marketplace unless we are taking part in an open-air service, and then we are just as likely to be embarrassed as proud. And as for disfiguring our faces when we fast—well, frankly, most of us probably don't ever fast, so the issue doesn't arise. Is there then no application of this passage to the present day? Far from it.

First, we need to be quite sure about fasting, prayer and giving. Is it always true that in our giving, the left hand doesn't know what the right hand is doing? I grant you that with many of us we are so haphazard about our giving that the *right* hand doesn't know what the right hand is doing. But is there a chance that we might be glad to be observed slipping a bit of cash into the collection? One of the good things about having a collection is that everyone puts something in, or if they don't other people shouldn't notice. It doesn't set one person apart from others. But we need to watch out here nonetheless.

What of prayer? Does it need saying that extempore prayer is always open to the danger of exhibitionism? Which is a good reason, incidentally, for using set prayers in church as a general rule. And do watch out for one of Satan's subtle tricks here. At one prayer meeting we may be moved from the heart to pray at length. We're not thinking about ourself at all: we're thinking about God, and about the matter we are bringing before him. But at the next prayer meeting when we pray, we may simply remember how well we put the phrases together, how much we enjoyed the sound of our own earnest, pious voice.

What about fasting? I suspect those who do fast properly are already sensitive to these warnings. But what about the pride that creeps in because of the things we have given up to do God's work? The time we have given up to go to those extra meetings? The luxuries we have done without in order to give to Tear Fund or Christian Aid? Splendid to give things up for God's work, but it is always dangerous to be too glad we did it.

As for straining out gnats and swallowing camels, I suppose that is a very characteristic evangelical disease. We tithe the mint and dill and cummin—we may be scrupulously careful about how we spend Sunday, we may never go to the theater, we may have a regular quiet time, which we never miss (and incidentally, what about the evangelical Pharisee who comes down late for breakfast and announces over the cold tea that he has been reading his Bible?), we may know how to dot the i's and cross the t's of the finer points of doctrine—and then when it comes to the weightier matters of the law, we fall flat on our faces. Think about them: *justice* (when so much injustice still cries out to be put right, and not just the current trendy "causes") and *love* (when every evangelical church has its own little circle of backbiting, bickering and party squabbles). No church can claim to be free of the error of the Pharisees. In fact, if it did, that itself would be evidence against it.

On the level of structures and patterns the story is pretty much the same. How many good evangelical churches quietly forget that in the New Testament the church appears to have attached a good deal of importance to baptism and holy Communion? Worse, how many realize but do not care it is forgotten (as long as our familiar patterns of worship are left as they are) or that the central service, the thing Jesus commanded us to do in remembrance of him, is shuffled around from week to week so that the whole church never meets around the Lord's Table? The little things are important, but only in the context of the big things. The gold in the temple is important, but only because the temple is more important. When we wash the outside of the cup, let it be because we have already washed the inside.

All right, so we are all hypocrites. But before we move on to see what Jesus says we should do about this, we must make some distinctions on the basis of Jesus' analysis of hypocrisy. Let me repeat what I said before: there are some things the world calls hypocrisy which are inevitable for the Christian. They are even to be welcomed. And it is important to make this distinction between (if you like) good hypocrisy and bad hypocrisy, because if we don't we will be thinking there is something in our life to put right when there isn't. And that is a recipe not only for frustration but also, pushed to extremes, for breakdown.

One of the things the world calls hypocrisy is doing things we do not really want to do at the time. Unless we really want to do it, we are hypocritical if we go through the motions.

However, if we live by that rule, we may never be a hypocrite, but we will be inconsistent, disobedient, selfish, unstable and ungodly. Should we only keep the Ten Commandments when we feel like keeping them? Just because our feelings change with the weather, must our moral standards do so too? These days we make a great fuss over so-called sincerity—always being true to our mood of the moment—and it rubs off on a lot of Christians who mistake this for what Jesus is saying in Matthew 5–6. But Jesus is not talking about feelings. He is talking about God's law and how we keep it from the heart. If God says, for example, we must pray regularly, then we must pray regularly: and one of the things we may need to pray for is that God will bring our heart and feelings into line with what we already know to be our basic duty.

"Duty!" says someone. "Isn't that just 'putting it on'?" In a way it is. And if we don't "put on" God's holiness when we feel like being unholy, then we have guarded our sincerity at the cost of our obedience. That is why I say that there is a hypocrisy the Christian has to welcome. Paul tells us to "put on" Christ, and often it is only as we obey, out of the knowledge that this is God's will, that the feelings come grudgingly into place. How often does a Christian begin to read the Bible without any real desire to do so, but only out of duty, and then discover that desire and delight follow behind duty rather than leading it on? We need to live in this tension, because this is what being a Christian is all about. It is what Paul calls the flesh lusting against the Spirit and the Spirit against the flesh. If living with this tension is hypocrisy, then every Christian is called to be a hypocrite.

The great modern idol of sincerity—the view that all that matters is doing what we feel like doing at the moment—is a classic example of scaling down ethics to fit fallen human nature. Its epitaph has been written recently in the posthumous autobiography of a member of Parliament who revealed that, as well as being a well-known churchman, he was also sexually promiscuous. In the book he acknowledges his inconsistency of behavior, but justifies it by saying that both in his churchgoing and in his perversion he was *always doing what he most wanted to do at the time.* That is only a justification for such behavior in a world that has lost its grip entirely on absolute standards and, paradoxically, on true human nature itself. God did not make us animals, that we should set our course by the changing wind of our instincts. He made us human beings so we could grasp his will with our minds, set *our* wills to obey it and tell our instincts to fall into line whether they like it or not. There is no shame for the Christian in the so-called hypocrisy of wanting to do one thing and in fact doing another because it is God's will. This hypocrisy is in any case only temporary. One of heaven's joys will be that there we will have no more tension between inclinations and obedience.

We must, then, make a distinction between different kinds of hypocrisy. The Pharisees' hypocrisy consisted in doing things in order to get human praise, and in concentrating on the small, finicky matters of obedience in order to avoid the big ones. But there is nothing wrong with the hypocrisy (so-called) that struggles to obey God's commandments whether it wants to or not. In fact if we do not do that, then we are becoming Pharisees ourselves. We are setting a higher value on what others think (that sincerity is what counts) than on what God thinks (that obedience, or the desire and struggle for obedience, is what counts). We are exchanging the praise that comes from our own day for the praise that comes from God.

A warning is necessary at this point in case anyone reading this out of context should think that I have abandoned the doctrine of justification by faith and settled instead for some sort of justification by obedience. I have not. In fact the view I have been attacking, this cult of "sincerity," is a modern perversion of faith. Christian obedience is not done in order to earn favor with God; nothing we can do, not even our faith or our sincerity, can earn that favor. It is God's gracious gift. It was the Pharisees who thought that they could earn God's favor by good deeds. When we struggle to obey God, we are not doing it because we are trying to earn anything but because God has already accepted us, and so—as forgiven children of a loving father, which is what Matthew 6 is all about—we begin to want to obey him. It is hard, and often unsuccessful, but that doesn't matter because we weren't earning anything by it anyway. What matters is that our wills begin to be orientated toward God, and that we show our gratitude for our free salvation by living as his willing children.

Back to Matthew 6. What is Jesus' remedy for pharisaic hypocrisy? The key words are *your Father* and *in secret*. What matters is that we are not trying to earn praise from anyone. We are to be dear children of a dear Father, glad to do his will whether or not anyone else knows about it. Do your almsgiving (v. 4), your praying (v. 6), your fasting (v. 18) secretly. Take Jesus literally, go into your room, shut the door and pray to your Father who sees in secret. What we are in secret is what we really are. If the secret place does not hear your prayer, then what people hear outside may very well come under the judgment of verse 5. The focus of all Christian piety is God, God our holy Father, and the only way to be sure we are fixing our mind on God is to live for him secretly. Is not one of the most fruitful points of Christian growth the battle we fight for the Lord but about which we never tell a soul? The old hymn "God Our Deliverer" says:

> Fear him, ye saints,
> and you will then
> have nothing else to fear;
> Make you his service your delight;
> your wants shall be his care.

That is why, in the middle of Matthew 6, we find the Lord's Prayer. It is God-centered, as all praying and living should be. It emphasizes our weakness, our dependence on God and our constant and daily need for forgiveness. I haven't space to develop this here, and in any case it is more something that we should all develop by doing it, not by talking or writing about it. I think we need to rediscover the Lord's Prayer, to take it out of its over-familiarity and actually use it as the foundation of all our praying. And in the context of hypocrisy it is exactly what we need. No one who prays this prayer day by day, and means it, is in any real danger of the Pharisees' pride. All who begin the day with it will go on their way knowing they are forgiven sinners, knowing their Father to be a loving and holy God. People like this have no need to put on a show before others. They live under the eye of God, who has already accepted them as his children and who, because he wants the best *for* them, also wants the best *from* them.

If that means that from time to time we feel as though we are "putting it on," and we have to obey God even though we would much rather do something else, then we have got good precedent for it. Jesus himself learned obedience by the things he suffered. And Jesus was no hypocrite. It is *his* life that God calls us to "put on," and, what is more, it is his Spirit who is given to enable us to know his will and do it, even if we still don't feel like it. (There are some who talk as if the Spirit's purpose was to make us *feel like* obeying God, but the Spirit is given to make us holy human beings, not satisfied animals.)

The whole thing therefore comes back to the basic principles of all Christian truth and all Christian living. Live your life under the eye of your loving Father. Struggle to obey him by the power of his Spirit. Model yourself on his incarnate Son, who himself fought with temptation, did things he didn't feel like doing (remember Gethsemane), and now sits at God's right hand, still clothed in our flesh and now triumphant. This path leaves no room for the hypocrisy of the Pharisee. It is only wide enough for those who do justice, love mercy and walk humbly with their God.

An old prayer sums all this up.

O God, forasmuch as without thee we are not able to please thee, mercifully grant that thy Holy Spirit may in all things direct and rule our hearts: through Jesus Christ, thy Son, our Lord. Amen.

11

THE RUNAWAY SLAVE

I ALWAYS FIND IT HARD TO understand why some people say they would have found the apostle Paul a difficult man to get on with. I grant you that he can't have been exactly a comfortable sort of person to have around the place. How would you like to be friends with a man who had been stoned by angry mobs, rejected by his own people and put in prison by the imperial authorities? And I suspect that when he spoke, much of what he said would have been far too deep and rich for most of us to appreciate more than a little of it. But difficult to get on with? I don't think so.

There is quite a bit of evidence. Why, for instance, did the Ephesian elders weep when Paul told them they would never see him again? One of the best examples of the impression Paul must have made on people is the short letter he wrote to Philemon, and I want to look at it here. We have been thinking in chapter ten how faith, true Christian faith, will often require us to do what God wants even when we don't feel like it. If we look between the lines of the letter to Philemon, we see more than one person in just that position.

Philemon lived at Colosse and was a well-known Christian who almost certainly had been converted through hearing Paul preach in Ephesus. His son, Archippus, seems to have been a minister in nearby Laodicea. Like all other families at the time, they had slaves who worked for them, and as often happened one of them had run away, probably helping himself to some family goods as he went. Even though Philemon was a Christian who was well-known for his love and generosity, no slave having done that would dare go near his old master again. Slaves were regularly crucified for less.

So what was the slave to do? If he had lived in present-day England, the answer would probably be, "go and lose yourself in London"; in the world of that day the obvious answer was, "go and lose yourself in Rome." But instead of getting lost when he went to Rome, Onesimus met Paul. Paul introduced him to Jesus. And Onesimus became a changed man. Instead of being a nobody, he knew that Jesus had died for him, to make him a child of God. Instead of being a mere runaway slave, he became a free man, free from his sin and his past.

But was he really free from his past? Jesus had forgiven him—but what about Philemon? Jesus had taught that it is no good being right with God if we are not reconciled with others. So Onesimus—and Paul—were in a very delicate position. How were they to approach Philemon? Paul set to work on what must be one of the most diplomatic, gentle and tactful of his or any letters. It is a shining example of the way Christian love—that is, faith turning into love—breaks down barriers between people. As such, it has things to teach us at all sorts of levels: in personal relationships, in ecumenical negotiations, in problems between different races and so on. Let's look at each of the three main characters in the story and see what their problems were and how they faced them.

First, Paul. The letter, as I said, is a model of tact and courtesy. Unlike some of his other letters, he does not begin by reminding the recipient of his credentials as an apostle (as he had to, for instance, in writing to the Galatians, when his very status was being challenged). He wants to make it quite clear that he is not laying down the law to Philemon but appealing to him out of love. He knows that if Philemon is going to respond and take Onesimus back it must be out of a willing heart, with no grudging or feeling of "Oh well, all right then." Philemon may have to begin from a position of not wanting to do what Paul says, but Paul aims at a wholehearted response in the end. So Paul makes it clear that he has a high opinion of Philemon and expects the best from him because he is the sort of Christian we *can* expect the best from. He sets Philemon an example. By not stressing his authority as an apostle, he shows Philemon the way to not stressing his rights as Onesimus's master.

He points out with extreme delicacy that Philemon owed him, Paul, his very soul, because it was through Paul that Philemon himself first heard the gospel, and says: "Very well, if *you* are my child in the gospel, then please accept from me another of my children in the gospel; if you and I are brothers in Christ, let us be glad to receive another brother in Christ."

Notice how Paul here copies Jesus himself. Philemon owed Paul his life, and so must receive Paul's messenger with the love due to Paul himself. The Christian owes Christ his life, and must remember that Jesus said to his disciples, "Whoever welcomes you welcomes me" (Matthew 10:40). Christ is at the center of Paul's life, and the love and tact and gentleness of this letter all flow from that fact. So too with us: we must not rush into instant solutions in relationships between individuals or churches, under the impression that because we ought to be reconciled this can and should be achieved by the wave of a magic wand. Such engineering can be extremely arrogant, ignoring the delicate and deeply felt problems that really exist. Like Paul, we must seek to win over others by the strength of our gentleness and the power of our Christlike love. Paul avoided the danger of arrogance by imitating Christ. His love was his faith in action.

How about poor Onesimus? He had quite the opposite problem. I am sure that in many ways he would much rather have stayed in Rome looking after Paul, as he apparently was doing already. But that wasn't any good. He had to learn, and put into practice, the fact that becoming a Christian affects all one's relationships. That meant facing up to his past.

He must have been frightened as he walked up the path to Philemon's house. Indeed, I think fear must have been the biggest thing he had to overcome. He had to learn to trust Christ for this as for everything. He was going back to remake an old relationship, but, more than that, to make a new one. And the

new one was to be a better but a harder one. A slave didn't
have to bother much about whether he loved his master or not.
But if he and his master were both Christians, there was a
much higher path to tread. In that position there would always
be the danger that one or the other would abuse the new relationship. Perhaps (he must have thought) Philemon wouldn't
like the idea of his return. Onesimus had to overcome fear,
simply through his faith in Christ, the Lord of the church and
hence of Philemon as well as himself.

We too, as we seek to be reconciled to individuals and
groups from whom we are estranged, need to trust the Lord
of the church, and not fear that we will be unwelcome, dominated or overpowered. There is always this danger about any
Christian relationship: because it must be free and loving,
there must always be the risk that one side will dominate, that
someone will get hurt. The only course is faith—faith, the
antidote to fear, the correlative of love. Faith is trusting God
despite appearances, on the basis of his known character. We
now see that love (love in action, not necessarily pleasant feelings about someone) is acting toward others on the basis of
that same character of God, the God of all—again, if need be,
despite appearances.

The problem facing Philemon was, in my opinion, altogether the hardest of the three. He may well have felt a bit
peeved that Onesimus, having run away from his Christian
household, had nonetheless become a Christian through Paul
(just as Christian parents are tempted to feel peeved when
their children learn from a stranger some things that the par-

ents had been trying unsuccessfully to teach them for years). Philemon had to learn to swallow his pride and trust God that Onesimus would not take advantage of his new, restored position. He also needed to forgive him for what he had done in the past.

Here is the heart of the matter. A kindly man might say, "We'll let bygones be bygones—let's see if the lad can turn over a new leaf." But Paul is clearly expecting something more from Philemon than a sort of happy-go-lucky readiness to forget the past and hope it'll all work out somehow. He tells Philemon (vv. 5-6) that he is praying for him, thanking God for his faith in Jesus Christ and his love for all God's people, and asking that the expression of his faith may become powerful in the knowledge of every good thing that is ours as we grow up into Christ. In other words, Paul wants Philemon to be a strong Christian, strong in knowing what the privileges and responsibilities of the Christian are, strong in putting them into practice.

Paul is here using a similar idea to that which he expresses in Ephesians 4, talking about the unity of Christians. He says that we are not to be like children, tossed to and fro and carried this way and that with every new idea that comes along. Rather, he says, we are to speak the truth in love and so grow up in every way into him who is the head, that is, Christ. This is very important for settling disagreements between Christians and churches. We are not to go along with every idea that comes up, as though doctrine doesn't matter provided we are all one big happy family. Instead, we are to speak the *truth* in *love* and grow up into Christ that way and no other.

Paul tells Philemon that this will happen as he knows more about all the good things that are ours as Christians. This cuts clean across a very popular idea today that suggests we ought not to stress the points on which we differ but rather come together with Christians from different backgrounds by agreeing on a sort of lowest-common-denominator Christianity—a sort of vague and watery commitment to Christ with no clear lines of doctrine at all. But that isn't growing up into Christ: if anything it is growing down, away from the fullness of truth contained in him.

Nor is it Christian love. It's a pale shadow of it, a sort of semi-Christian version of the current idea of tolerance, which comes to mean that we don't much care what anyone believes as long as they don't believe it too firmly. What Paul is recommending to Philemon is the sort of love that has the courage to look all the differences and difficulties full in the face—to refuse to accept a half-hearted "Oh, all right then" attitude. This sort of love lays its cards on the table and expects others to do the same. Such Christians are humble enough to do it because they know that Jesus has forgiven them, and they are brave enough to do it because they know that the other person, living under the same Lord, will love and respect them despite their differences.

Therefore, if we are to come together as Christians, it will not be by watering down everything until there is so little left that we can all agree on it. It will be by all of us learning more and more of Christ, and of the truth about him, so that we can grow closer to each other because we are closer to him.

I have seen this work out in practice. When I was a delegate at the 1975 Assembly of the World Council of Churches, I found over and over again that it was when we said what we really meant, expressing ourselves and our viewpoints most clearly, that real fellowship and trust came about—not when we hid the light of truth under a bushel of tolerance. After all, whoever heard of a family or a married couple who were happy to say that they simply tolerated each other? In a Christian marriage and family the members don't aim simply at coexistence with the minimum fuss. They face problems and difficulties, seeking to go on loving one another while they work through the problem to the other side. As Paul says in verse 5 of his letter to Philemon, the love which the Christian has for all brothers and sisters in Christ is based on the faith he or she has in Jesus. That faith is precisely the faith that God has loved us with an everlasting love, and that in Christ he has loved us to the uttermost. The love of God is the substance of our faith, and must therefore be the primary characteristic of our lives. God's love is the sort that looks at the worst in us and loves us just the same. And in our love of one another, as individuals and as members of different Christian groups and churches, we dare not aim at anything else.

The story of Philemon and Onesimus ends without our knowing what happened. We hope, of course, that they were reconciled and that Paul was able to visit them as he wanted to. But we don't know. (We do hear, some time later, of a man called Onesimus being a bishop in Ephesus.) As a result, the letter appears incomplete, and it is up to Christians in every age to complete it themselves. We must take up the threads ourselves and allow our faith in Christ to grow and mature into Christlike love.

12

WHEN FRIENDS FALL OUT

A BIG TRIUMPH IS OFTEN FOLLOWED by a petty tragedy.

It is one of the enduring features of any Christian work that when Christians have worked and prayed their way through a problem or a difficult task, and seen it safely to a conclusion, they no sooner breathe a sigh of relief than they find themselves tripped up by something small and comparatively insignificant. The person who preaches a brilliant sermon may go home and be unkind to her spouse. The man who pioneers a major work of love in action may fall down in his relationships with his close colleagues. It should not be so, but how often it is. And it is to Luke's credit that when it happens to Paul, he doesn't gloss it over. It is a sad little story, but we can learn quite a bit from it, particularly in the whole area of faith-turning-into-love that we have been thinking about.

It happened immediately after the apostolic council recorded in Acts 15. Paul and Barnabas, fresh from their missionary journeys together, had successfully presented to the

Jerusalem gathering their view of the Gentile mission: Gentiles should be allowed to become Christians without first becoming Jews, without (that is) needing to be circumcised. This great principle of the gospel—that all are on an even footing before God—stands at the heart of Paul's theology as we find it in Romans and Galatians, being based on the fact that God is one (see, for instance, Romans 3:27-30). Paul could look on the Jerusalem meeting with satisfaction. Against those who said the Gentiles had to be circumcised in order to be Christians, he had safeguarded the truth that God's grace knows no racial distinction.

Perhaps he did look on it with satisfaction. And perhaps that was just the problem. Because right away he and Barnabas, who had worked together, preached together, prayed together, suffered together, fought side by side for the defense and spread of the gospel, had a full-scale row. Paul wanted to revisit the churches they had founded, and Barnabas wanted to take Mark with them. But Mark had abandoned their earlier journey before it had hardly begun, and Paul was simply not going to have him with them again. Both insisted that they were right. Luke records simply that "They had such a sharp disagreement that they parted company" (Acts 15:39 NIV). Barnabas began a journey of his own, keeping to his plan of taking Mark. Paul went off on his intended venture, this time taking Silas. It is all very sad, and very true to life.

But whose fault was it? Which one of them was in the wrong? That is not an easy question to answer. We need to look at both men and try to see the matter through their eyes.

Barnabas first: he was the senior man, the older as a Christian, the leader to begin with on the first journey, even regarded as such when it became clear that Paul had the greater speaking gifts. He had been one of Paul's first Christian friends—the man who had believed in the ex-Pharisee when others were suspicious of him, and who had introduced him to the Jerusalem apostles (Acts 9:27). He was part of one of the original Christian families. Being Mark's cousin (Colossians 4:10), he was also probably related to Peter. His aunt, Mark's mother, lived in Jerusalem, where her house was one of the focal points of the early church (Acts 12:12). Can it be that the gentle Barnabas had in him just a touch of pride lying under the surface until brought out by Paul's attempt to tell him to leave his cousin behind? Maybe all along Barnabas had—no doubt subconsciously—been pleased that his family should be taking the lead in this exciting new way of life that was beginning to turn the world upside down. Maybe all along—again no doubt without realizing it—he had regarded Paul simply as an excellent number two.

On the other hand, didn't Barnabas have a point? He probably knew Mark as well as anyone, and may well have known that Mark was ashamed of his earlier behavior and ready now to prove himself if given a second chance. What business has a Christian to stifle a young man who sees his weaknesses and is eager to show that he is overcoming them? After all, Christian work is not meant to be done without thought for the needs, the spiritual growth and the maturity of the workers who are doing it. Maybe Barnabas was simply bending over backward to try to exercise just that sort of reconciling love Paul was later to urge on Philemon.

Then what of Paul? Was he being wildly inconsistent with his own principles as stated in the letter to Philemon and in, for instance, 1 Corinthians 13 and Philippians 2? Much of the evidence seems to suggest that he was. Maybe he had looked down his nose at Mark for hurrying off back to Jerusalem even before the going got tough. (It was after Mark had gone back to his mother's house that Paul and Barnabas ran into the real trouble [Acts 13:50; 14:5, 19].) Maybe he had been pleased with his own performance as a roving evangelist—and who wouldn't be, blazing a trail across Asia Minor with a revolutionary message, thinking thoughts that no one had thought before, discovering theological truths in theory and in practice, seeing people converted as he spoke. He must have been absolutely delighted with the result of the Jerusalem conference, with the top brass coming around to his way of thinking in the end. Like Barnabas, maybe he had come to regard the work as *his* work. He had done it. God had used him in this way before. He was the man with the experience. He knew that only the tough could survive on the mission field. And all along God is saying, Paul, it isn't your work. It isn't your church. Barnabas, it isn't yours either. God alone owns the growing church, and like a father with two squabbling children, he needs to teach them both a sharp lesson.

On the other hand, wasn't Paul perfectly correct? He couldn't know for sure that the churches he had planted had flourished. They might have been swept away or driven into hiding by persecution, and going back might have been more dangerous than the first trip. He couldn't know that this second journey would go distances that made the first one look like an afternoon stroll. When we are facing the unknown, better to go with people we can trust. If we are going to have a threefold cord, better that each strand should be equally strong.

It may be an uncomfortable answer to the question, but it does begin to look as though Paul and Barnabas were both in the wrong—and both in the right. And isn't that true to life as well? Disputes are fairly easy to settle when one person is in the right and the other is in the wrong. But most quarrels are not like that. Paul and Barnabas arguing about Mark is typical of so many of us. Barnabas couldn't let go of his point: God's work is not to go on by means of weaker individuals being thrown on the scrap heap. All have a place in his service. But Paul couldn't let go of his: there are stern warnings for those who put their hand to the plough and then turn back. There is no sense in putting a weak link in a chain that is going to bear a lot of weight, just so that the link doesn't feel left out.

Did they have to have their fight, then? Was there no way out?

Perhaps in one sense there wasn't. A quarrel is usually the last stage in a long process. To avoid it we would have to turn the clock back and eradicate the subconscious pride and arrogance that had built up in both parties. From that point of view the quarrel had to happen sooner or later, and perhaps it was just as well that it happened when it did and not miles away on the mission field where it might have done untold harm. To that extent we can see God's providence, I think, in bringing matters to a head while they were still in Antioch.

But from another point of view, which we would do well to ponder, there was no need for the quarrel at all. Just because two people are sure they are right, and their opinions appear to be different, there is no automatic need for them to get steamed up with each other. If they do, the steam does not come from the disagreement itself but from personal factors—pride, arrogance, fear of being dominated or fear of losing face. These things simply take over and use the outward agreement as a convenient battleground.

Thus the argument between Paul and Barnabas, while superficially about Mark, was (at a much deeper level) about Paul and Barnabas. This is evidenced by the fact that there was a simple solution to the question of Mark—which in fact was adopted by a painful route, though it could just as easily have been agreed amicably. Two journeys instead of one! Why hadn't they thought of that before? Barnabas can go somewhere reasonably civilized, where there is less risk, and take Mark with him to break him in more gently to the idea of traveling missionary work. Cyprus? An ideal place. Barnabas came from there in the first place, and on their first visit (Mark still with them at this stage) the governor himself had been converted. Little chance of persecution there. Paul can go north, which is through his home territory anyway, and another new man can join the work.

How easy it would have been in theory to reach this conclusion, but for the unwillingness of both men to give an inch. Paul argues that black is black, Barnabas that white is white, and both, knowing they are right, fail to see that in God's purpose there is plenty of room for both and for several shades in between. The squabble was not necessary in the sense of being a necessary condition for the accomplishment of God's purposes in the missionary work. It may have been necessary in order to make Paul and Barnabas face up to themselves, but that is a very different thing. The biggest tragedy that can happen in that sort of situation is when this result is not achieved, and each party goes off still convinced of his or her own correctness and of the other person's pigheadedness. It is to be hoped—and in view of what Paul could later write I believe it is true—that both men did realize that when our ideas conflict with somebody else's, God's ideas may be on a larger scale. He may well have room for both.

Was God in control over the whole episode? Some people talk as if God loses control when people sin. But that isn't what this story tells me. God didn't cause the sin, of course! God, still sovereign over his fallen creation, brings about two missionary journeys instead of one. He provides a gentle rehabilitation for Mark; he brings forward Silas, a man with the trust of the Jerusalem church and (most important for the next journey) a Roman citizen, to share the work with Paul; he gives Paul his head, with nothing to hold him back from evangelizing his way right into Europe. All this could have been achieved without the bitterness; yet even this can be used in God's purpose. God, in bringing to a head the latent pride and arrogance in the two men, not only averted a disaster, he alerted both to their own weakness. He often needs to do the same today.

Over the whole sad story stands the God whose great purposes we have begun to explore in this book. It is faith in him, once again, that we need when things go wrong on a personal level, as on any other. When we determine to see our personal plans and hopes in the light of his will and that alone, and recognize that his will is always far bigger than our understanding of it, then there is no need to be arrogant or fearful toward anyone else. That is why faith and love are two sides of the same coin. When we see the love of God and the sovereignty of God (and what is faith but looking at the loving King of heaven, as we were doing at the beginning of the book?), we are in the right position to submit to one another with humility and dignity. Read Philippians 2 again—right through to the end—and consider the path by which Paul himself had reached the conclusions which he there commends.

13

THE MOTHERS' MEETING

MARY HAD A SECRET. IN ONE WAY, of course, it was, and is, a very common and natural secret for a young woman to have. But in Mary's case it was a bit different. For a start, for most young women the news that they are going to have a baby isn't normally brought by a messenger from heaven. And for another thing, while most young mothers may dream of a wonderful life ahead for their child, Mary had been told that the child she was going to have was to be none other than the Son of God, who would reign as a King over the people of God.

With any news that big, the last thing you want to do is to tell everybody about it, but the first thing you want to do is probably to tell somebody about it. So Mary got ready quickly and set off to see her cousin, who she knew would be a good person to talk to. In any case, one of the things the angel had said to her was that Elizabeth—who was well past the usual age for having children—was expecting a baby as well. So she just had to see Elizabeth.

So off she went on her journey—about the distance from London to Birmingham—and the journey's end is the mothers' meeting. And what a meeting! One of the most marvelous mothers' meetings that the people of God have ever had. Here it is (from Luke 1:39-45, freely translated): Mary went into the house and greeted Elizabeth with her news. And when Elizabeth heard what Mary said, the baby gave a jump in her womb, and Elizabeth was filled with the Holy Spirit, and exclaimed in a loud voice:

> Blessed are you among women, and blessed is the fruit of your womb. And why has this happened to me, that the mother of my Lord comes to me? For as soon as I heard the sound of your greeting, the child in my womb leaped for joy. And blessed is she who believed that there would be a fulfillment of what was spoken to her by the Lord.

The background to this story is two thousand or so years of Jewish history, going back to Abraham. Throughout that two thousand years the Jewish people had lived by faith in the promise of God that one day—one day—God would send a child of Abraham who would not only redeem Israel but also be a light to lighten all the nations of the world. Mary looked back to the years of tradition which had prepared her race, and her in particular, for this one all-important event. All the lessons God had taught his people in the past were now to be summed up in the baby that she was to have.

But look now at the two women's response to the news. Two things really shine out of this passage, and the first is their utter humility. It is very touching; there is never for a moment any suggestion of the thought, *I must be a terribly important person if after all these years God is going to work out his purposes through* me. On the contrary, Mary is humility itself. "Here I am, the servant of the Lord," she had said. She didn't know what God was doing, but only that she belonged to him and was ready for whatever he was planning. And Elizabeth too has no trace of jealousy about her. She is simply amazed and overjoyed at being allowed to be in on the purposes of God at all. There is no suggestion that she is cross because her son will not be as important as Mary's. A marvelous example, this, of the way that being absorbed with God's purposes prevents that jealousy which so easily springs up between two families when they are related and both having a baby. They are both humble before God. After centuries of planning, his purposes are being worked out through them, and their only thought is of how undeserving they are.

The second thing is their faith. It is faith that Elizabeth puts her finger on as being the key to why Mary is called blessed. It is not just her privilege that makes her blessed: the privilege was going to involve her in a lot of suffering as well as a great deal of joy. It was the faith which had heard God promising the impossible and had believed him. Blessed is she, says Elizabeth, who *believed* that there would be a fulfillment of those things spoken to her by the Lord. Just as Abraham, two thousand years before, had been told by God that he and Sarah would have a son, impossible though it was in human terms because they were so old, and Abraham had believed God, so

his descendant Mary is told by God that she will have a son,
even though she has no husband, and she believes him.

It is not, of course, simply believing the impossible, as some
would make out today. It is knowing the character of God,
that he is the Creator, the one who specializes (so to speak) in
giving life where there is none. It is this same character of God
that is at work in the resurrection of Jesus; and it is the same
life-giving power that as Christians we rely on to give life to
us when we first become Christians out of our natural state of
death (see Ephesians 2:1-10) and when we need his help day by
day. Mary is "blessed" because she believed in just this power
of God to fulfill his promises in new and unexpected ways—
to give life where there was none.

This faith, and this humility, are to sustain and mark out
God's people in every age. We fortunate Christians in this
century can look back gladly and rightly to centuries of tradition, to centuries of men and women who served God faith-
fully and who trusted him to keep his promises. We must now
be ready, like Mary, to continue that tradition by trusting God
to do new things among us. What new things is God doing in
the world today? Are we ready to be part of them? The danger,
of course, with traditions is that they go dead on us. But our
God is a God who is always breathing new life into old structures and traditions, and making them alive with the presence
of Christ even as he made Mary's womb alive with that same
sacred presence.

This will mean different things to each person who reads
these words. But the constant factor for everybody is this: as

God had a purpose for Mary, so he has a unique purpose for each one of his children, and for them all together as a community. And just as that purpose involved Mary in obedient submission to his will, so it will involve us in that same readiness to say, "Not my will, but thine." Just as Mary did not understand how God could possibly do what he had promised, and yet believed, so we may well have to shake our heads at our circumstances, our prospects, our whole lives, and say in faith to God: "Father, I don't understand you, but I trust you." That is what faith is all about.

This may lead us, in obedient faith, into some fresh form of service for God—something we could do in our spare time, some talent or gift to be set aside for his glory. (I am not here talking about the "willing horses" in every church, the small handful who do most of the hard work already and cram every spare second with it—except to suggest to them that one of God's unexplored purposes for them might actually lie at home. Rather, I am talking to those—the majority of Christians—who haven't yet realized the joy of hearing God's call to serve him, to share in his fresh purposes for his people, and obeying it.) Obedient faith may well lead us, quietly and humbly, to work a bit harder at getting on with some relative or friend, or member of our own household, who we find it difficult to live with at the moment. Remember Mary and Elizabeth—no pride in Mary, no jealousy in Elizabeth, but rather both perfectly submitted to God's will. Leave the rebukes to God; our part is to give ourself in love.

In all this I am saying, let Christ be formed in you, as he was in Mary, so that as Elizabeth rejoiced to meet Mary, so others may rejoice to meet and know you and your church. Not for nothing is Mary, the mother of Jesus, the pattern of the church which, says Paul (Galatians 4:26), is the mother of us all. We must set ourselves to live as she did—by obedient faith in the life-giving God, within the context of the history that has brought us where we are, watching for the new things that our God is doing today.

14

FAITH FOR A WEDDING

WHAT I HAVE TO SAY HERE IS NOT really long enough to be a chapter on its own, but I could hardly leave it out of a section about biblical faith turning into love. As we might expect, God's pattern for married love is the highlight of the biblical view of love. One of the best known passages on the subject is Ephesians 5:21-33, and there are many things that could be said about it. Here I just want to point out two implications of the picture Paul draws there, in which marriage is likened to the relationship Jesus Christ has with his people, his bride, the church.

First, it means that at every point of marriage there is before a Christian couple—or anyone who wants to look at it—a clear picture of how they are to love each other. Husbands, says Paul, you must love your wives just as Christ loved the church. What does that mean? It means that he went to the greatest depth for the church, dying on the cross to save and purify her. Christ loved us, as we know, when we were totally unworthy of his love. The pattern for marriage is that we don't remain faithful to each other because the partner has earned it, but simply because we *will* go on loving them. When the husband says "I love you," he shouldn't mean simply, "I feel good when I think about you," but "I am yours, committed to you, determined to help you, support you, comfort you and even suffer for you, as long as we both live." Of course the word *love* has been grossly devalued by popular usage, but that is what it means in the biblical pattern. Christ's love for the church is no passing emotion that comes and goes with the weather. It is a total commitment, including the emotions of course, but ready to carry on regardless when the emotions are, for whatever reason, out of sorts.

Once we see this, we realize that, for the wife, the obedience to which she is called (Paul says, "as the church is subject to Christ, so also wives ought to be, in everything, to their husbands" [v. 24]) is certainly not a matter of being her husband's slave, as some have mistakenly thought. The church is not the slave of Christ in that sense! He has set her free, free to be truly herself in the context of his love. The church is right to obey Christ, even when he asks difficult or unexpected things of her—because he never asks anything of her that he is not facing himself, that is not for her greatest good and joy, and that he will not himself help her to accomplish. When a marriage works like that, it will be working according to its maker's intentions, and husband and wife will find that they are free to be themselves in the context of each other's love. Love does not smother its object. By giving it true security, it sets it free.

Second, the picture has an implication in the opposite direction. Human love in turn teaches us things about divine love. The sheer gladness of a wedding day is only a pale reflection of the joy and delight that come, and will come fully one day, to those who truly belong to Christ's people. When a husband finds it difficult to love his wife through a particular crisis, he may reflect on the fact that Christ's love met and conquered far harder obstacles than any we face. When a wife trusts and obeys her husband in some matter, she may reflect on the same obedience that is required of her as a Christian. Of course, not all wives deserve such love, and not all husbands deserve such obedience. But this is the pattern to aim at. When we experience the rich and wonderful joys of marriage, we may reflect that Christ has in store for those who love him joys and pleasures that will put all that in the shade.

15

THE HEART OF THE MATTER

I was involved in a mission in Oxford some years ago. It was a marvelous occasion. As so often, the message that came out of it was an old one, which gained freshness from the obvious depth and faith of the speaker. The aim of being a Christian, he said, is to know God and make him known.

Now in biblical terms to "know" someone often means much more than it does to us. For us, knowing someone often simply means knowing them well enough to say hello when we see them in the street. But knowing God isn't like that. To "know" in the Bible very often means to have a deep, close, warm relationship with someone. That puts the missioner's statement in a rich light indeed. The aim of being a Christian is—to love God and make him loved.

Through this section we have been thinking about how faith turns into love—how knowing what God is like, knowing what he has done for us in and through Jesus, produces in us love for those around us. Now we must sum it all up by looking at the love of God himself, since in fact when we talk about loving God there is no human love which will serve as a model for us to use. Nothing else than God's love for us will serve as a pattern for our love for him. This is the biblical way of looking at the matter. As John says, we love him because he first loved us.

Perhaps the obvious place to begin is Deuteronomy, in a passage that shows the similarity between the two loves and also the fact that our love for God is totally dependent on his for us:

> It was not because you were more numerous than any other people that the LORD set his heart on you and chose you—for you were the fewest of all peoples. It was because the LORD loved you and kept the oath that he swore to your ancestors. (Deuteronomy 7:7-8)

In other words, God's love is its own cause. The people of God can never look at themselves and say, "God loves us because we are like this or this." Neither our good works nor our fine characteristics nor even our faith itself can ever become a qualification for the love of God. So when Paul wants to assure us that God does indeed love us, he points not to anything in ourselves but to the actions that God has taken on our behalf. God, he says, did not spare his own Son, but gave him up to death on our behalf. God's love can only be measured against the immeasurable cost of Calvary.

Calvary shows us that we were utterly *undeserving* of God's love. Our plight was so desperate that nothing but the death of

God's Son, in our place and on our behalf, could provide a remedy. Calvary shows us that God in his love was nevertheless utterly *determined* to save sinful men and women from their sin. His heart was set on it: as Paul says in Romans 5:8, God commends his love to us in that, while we were yet sinners, Christ died for us. And Calvary shows us that God in his love will remain utterly *dependable*. If he loved us that much while we were his enemies, how much easier, more natural, more joyful will be his Easter love for us now that we are reconciled! This is at the heart of the matter, because it reveals to us the heart of God. If we want to know what his love is like, look at Calvary and we will see (in the words of William Cowper):

Mine is an unchanging love,
Higher than the heights above,
Deeper than the depths beneath,
Free and faithful, strong as death.

Nothing, says Paul (Romans 8:39) can separate us from the love of this God, our God. If you have never felt or known the sheer power or strength of God's love, take another look at Jesus dying on the cross. That was where mercy and truth really did meet together, because our forgiveness was not achieved by God's mercy ignoring the true facts about our sinful condition, but rather by his dealing with them in the only possible way. As John Donne wrote: "whom God loves, he loves to the end: and not only to their own end, to their death, but to his end, and his end is that he might love them still."

We can now begin to see how it is that Deuteronomy can do something that, to our modern ideas about love, seems extremely peculiar. In Deuteronomy 6 we are actually *commanded* to love God. This is surely because in the Bible we are not told to fall in love with God in the way that one might fall in love, almost casually and often without really thinking about it, with another person. We are simply told to love God and (almost naively simply) told to love him with all our heart and soul and might (Deuteronomy 6:5, quoted by Jesus in Matthew 22:37). And this is not an injunction to do the impossible, to stir up out of nothing feelings and emotions of love toward God. It is an invitation to look at who God is, at what he has done for us and at what he promises to do for us. For the children of Israel, that meant looking at their God, the one true God, who had delivered them from Egypt and would bring them home into the Promised Land. For us it means, I suggest, looking at the same God of Israel, now made known fully and finally in Jesus, who died for us and now guarantees our salvation. In the light of this, the invitation to love him begins to make sense. Not to love this loving God would be, to say the least, the grossest ingratitude.

In fact this love, like every other aspect of salvation, is not intended to be the candidate's own unaided work. Paul writes in Romans 8: "the Spirit helps us in our weakness; for we do not know how to pray as we ought [and what is prayer but the stirrings within us of love for God?], but that very Spirit intercedes [for us]" (v. 26). And Paul goes on at once, we know that all things work together for good—*to those that love God*. God demonstrates his love for us by the gift of his Son. He enables us to love him in return by the gift of his Spirit. If your heart and soul and strength remain unaffected by the death of God's Son on your behalf, then pray for the gift of the life-giving, love-giving Spirit.

I do not want to give you the impression that the love with which we are commanded to love God has nothing to do but silently adore him; although of course if it doesn't begin there, it is surely a pretty poor sort of thing. After all, if a wife says to her husband, "Do you love me?" and he replies, "Yes, my dear. I do the washing-up for you every day," that would only be a sensible or worthwhile answer if he meant that the washing-up was evidence of a love that in fact went far deeper. Love does not actually consist in washing up. But equally, if there were no such outward evidences, the wife might well wonder if the inner love was all it should be.

So it is with us and God. Significantly, in almost every place in Deuteronomy where we are commanded to love God, we are in the same breath told to keep his commandments. This is not an arbitrary thing, a malicious request designed to bring us into a sort of slavery. We can see that kind of thing in the story of Samson and Delilah. Delilah said to Samson: "If you really love me, you'd tell me why you're so strong," when all the time she wanted to hand him over to the Philistines. There have been some who actually thought that love and law were opposites, that the law was there to discover our weak points and enslave us as Delilah in fact succeeded in doing to Samson.

Not a bit of it. Listen again to Deuteronomy 6:5-7:

> You shall love the LORD your God with all your heart,
> and with all your soul, and with all your might. Keep
> these words that I am commanding you today in your
> heart. Recite them to your children and talk about them
> when you are at home and when you are away, when you
> lie down and when you rise.

If you are in any doubt which words these are—well, the
previous chapter contains the Ten Commandments for a start!
The law is not the opposite of love. The law is a true revelation
of God's holy character—as true a revelation of it as is Jesus
himself. And it was Jesus himself, on the night he was betrayed, who echoed Deuteronomy when he said to his disciples: if you love me, keep my commandments. Read John
13–14 and 1 John 3:1–5:5 if you want to pursue the matter
further. Keeping Jesus' commandments is no legalism. Having
seen the love of God, keeping his commandments is putting
our love for him into action.

Deuteronomy 6:8 says that this love, and this obedience,
are to be a sign on our hands, and as frontlets between our
eyes. Notice the little word *as*. We are not meant to do what
the Pharisees did and wear little boxes containing texts from
Scripture on our hands or our foreheads. We are rather to
settle it in our minds that whenever we turn our hand to any
task or activity, our obedient love for God will be at work in
and through that hand. We are to settle it in our minds that
whenever we turn our eyes to anything—or anyone—right

there between our two eyes, directing, controlling and purifying our gaze will be nothing less than our love for God and
our desire to please him. It is not only on the cross that love
and righteousness are to be mingled together.

Finally, we cannot speak of love for God without pointing
out that this is something we do not do just as individuals.
Archbishop Stuart Blanch, in *For All Mankind*, his little book
on the Old Testament, sums up the message of this part of
Deuteronomy by saying that no book of the Bible summons
the church more urgently to *be* the church. In other words,
if we are the people of God, then let us live like the people
of God. When people say they love God, but hate their
brother or sister, they are not telling the truth (1 John 4:20).
The new commandment Jesus gave, as he prepared to go
from the Upper Room to Gethsemane, and then to the cross,
was that the disciples should love one another as he loved
them (John 13:34).

We need to do some hard thinking here. The church has
been extraordinarily slow to take Jesus up on these words.
The world has yet to see what God will do through a worldwide church whose members love one another. We must work
together at this, praying for one another and particularly for
those we don't agree with. We are not called upon to compro-
mise our beliefs when we get together with others who do not
share them in every detail. We are called to submit our beliefs
to the acid test of whether in practice they show, by reproduc-
ing God's love in us, that they are inspired by his Spirit and
patterned on his Son.

Here is an old prayer you might like to use. It was written by E. B. Pusey, an Oxford theologian in the nineteenth century.

O God, fountain of love, pour thy love into our souls, that we may love those whom thou lovest with the love thou givest us, and think and speak of them tenderly, meekly, lovingly; and so loving our brethren and sisters for thy sake, may grow in thy love, and dwelling in thy love may dwell in thee; for Jesus Christ's sake. Amen.

part three

FAITH TO WALK
IN THE DARK

16

BETHLEHEM AND
THE BARLEY HARVEST

WE WALK BY FAITH, NOT BY SIGHT, and some of us don't like it that way.

Some of us are always wanting a bit more "sight" than God intends for us in this life, trying to get a bit of heaven here and now for which we are not yet ready. This last section of the book is going to see the way faith turns not only into love but also into hope. Each of the three is equally "not by sight": as Paul says, "hope that is seen is not hope" (Romans 8:24).

How do people want more sight than they should? We see the answer all over the church today. We see it in many people's attitude to prayer and to living the Christian life in general. Christians get frustrated that they do not see anything spectacular going on in their lives, such as they read about in the "Christian success story" kind of books. They have to walk by faith, not by sight, and they get disappointed. Have another look at those success stories: behind the spectacular moments there usually lie weeks, months, years of patient, undramatic waiting on God, reading the Bible, learning to pray, worshiping with fellow Christians, finding out how to live for God in the little things of life. Not the sort of stuff you write a book about. But very necessary as background work.

We see it too in many people's attitude to the church. I don't find in the New Testament any suggestion that the visible church ought to be composed of guaranteed 100 percent soundly converted keen Christians. If it had been, half the epistles would not have been necessary. Yet people are always hankering after a false security, such as we would get from belonging to a church that could be *seen* to be all right, *seen* to be "sound"—seen? We walk by faith, not by sight. Any attempt to get a purer church or purer Christian life than we have been promised this side of heaven runs the risk of attempting to base security, assurance of salvation, on something other than the free grace and love of God. It cannot be done. It must not be done. We walk by faith, not by sight.

Does this mean that we settle for second best? Certainly not. We make every effort to keep ourselves and the church free from sin and error. But we must never imagine that we have attained that standard or that we will in this life (see Philippians 3). The glory of the gospel is that this doesn't matter. We are not going to heaven because we now live perfect lives where before we didn't. That is legalism with the lid off. We are going to heaven, if by grace we are, only because of God's love shown on the cross. And that we know and receive only by faith.

We see the same hankering after a false security, the same desire for "sight," in churches where people grumble if the words or the ritual of the service are altered one little bit. We see it when Christians try to present the gospel to people by saying, "God loves you and has a wonderful plan for your life." That is quite true, but Jesus told his followers to take up their crosses and follow him through the valley of the shadow of death. We see it in the attitude that defines *sin* or *worldliness* in terms of various particular activities which, granted, might well be sinful for many people, but which themselves are indifferent (according to the Bible, that is [see Romans 14]). It is the same thing: Here is a neat little category of things you must not do. Keep the rules and you are all right. Break them and you are backsliding.

The trouble is that real Christianity is not like that. We walk by faith, not by sight. Of course there are the great ethical norms no sane Christian can think of breaking—murder, adultery and the rest. And of course there is disagreement between Christians as to which really are the important things and which the matters of indifference. But the attempt to get security by defining matters that are genuine points of disagreement between genuine Christians—that is an attempt to walk by sight. Real Christian living is much *harder* than that. Slapping labels on things may (possibly) be useful for children. It is not mature biblical Christian living.

What has all this got to do with Bethlehem and the barley harvest?

Just this: Ruth, in the first chapter of the book named after her, is a perfect example of someone refusing to walk by sight, and choosing instead to find her security only in God. This is faith looking at the future and trusting the great and loving God to guide it as he has the past. This is faith to walk in the dark, faith without sight.

The trouble with the first chapter of Ruth is that most of us know in advance how the story will end. We know that it all worked out happily, that Ruth got married and had children. But that was just what Ruth and Naomi did not know at the point where we join them. We have to think ourselves back into their position.

Here is Naomi, an old widow who badly wanted to be a grandmother—not for her own sake but so her family could be carried on—and who had seen every chance of this snatched away from her as her two sons died childless. She was bewildered, sad and bitter. Here is Ruth, a young widow, one of Naomi's daughters-in-law, eminently marriageable, yet torn between the desire to stay in her own country, Moab, and her desire to go with her aging mother-in-law into the unknown world of the Jews. In these two women we have a picture of the people of God in every age, under stress, in difficulty, troubled in spirit, unable to see what God is doing in their lives, feeling even that there is nothing left to live for. We may not be feeling like this at the moment. But it is better to learn in advance how God tests faith than to plunge into darkness first and then wonder what it means and how to cope with it.

Naomi looked at the darkness, and *knew that it was God's darkness*. She knew that the bitterness she was experiencing came from the hand of a loving Father. She doesn't say it all happened by chance or that the devil did all these awful things while God wasn't looking. She knew that the explanation of her present circumstances was with the one God, the Lord of Israel. Look at the text of Ruth 1. Naomi says, "The LORD has turned against me" (v. 13); "the Almighty has dealt bitterly with me" (v. 20); "The Lord has dealt harshly with me and the Almighty has brought calamity upon me" (v. 21). Naomi had learned the secret of faith in a sovereign, almighty God. Nothing is gained by pretending that difficulties happen without God knowing about them. What use is faith in a God who is always dropping off to sleep at the crucial moment?

Ruth picked up the same attitude from her mother-in-law. We might have thought that, for someone born as she was outside the people of Israel, there wouldn't be much attraction in the Jewish God who had apparently made Naomi's life a misery. But in fact Ruth was drawn irresistibly to this God who remains sovereign over all the affairs of his people, who somehow inspires trust without visible reasons. Perhaps he contrasted favorably with the moody and unreliable gods of her pagan background. Anyway, when Naomi offered her the chance of going back home to her family and *its* gods (v. 15), she refused. She must go with the people of the almighty God. "Where you go, I will go; where you lodge, I will lodge; your people shall be my people, and your God my God. Where you die I will die—there will I be buried" (vv. 16-17). She must go where Israel's God is honored, even if only to a grave. Ruth, like Naomi, walks by faith, not by sight.

The two women together give us a tremendous picture of biblical faith. It is faith that looks at a black past, and says, "God is almighty." It is faith that looks at a present without security, and says, "We belong to God's people." It is faith that looks at a future without prospects, and says, "God will provide." At the end of the chapter the two women arrive at Bethlehem with a hopeless future, but with an almighty God.

When all hope is gone, God reveals his plan. The chapter ends with the deceptively simple statement: "They came to Bethlehem at the beginning of the barley harvest" (v. 22). Bethlehem and the barley harvest: the place, the time and the means through which God was to provide a husband for Ruth and a family for Naomi. If ever we wanted an example of God's sovereign trustworthiness, we have one here. God's appointed husband for Ruth lived in Bethlehem, and as the two women arrived at the town, Boaz was getting ready for the harvest work through which God would bring them together. The heaviness has endured for a night, and the joy now comes in the morning.

We saw earlier how Ruth's faith expressed itself in terms of commitment to the people of God. It was not a solitary thing. We can now see, as we stand back from the picture a little, that God's solution to the problem brings with it blessing for his whole people as well. Think on for a moment to the end of the book. Ruth and Boaz had a son called Obed. Obed had a son called Jesse. And Jesse became the father of a splendid family, with a young son called David. In solving Ruth's and Naomi's very personal problems and griefs, God also began the family that would produce the King of Israel, the man after God's own heart. God's plans for individuals, for his whole people and for the world dovetail together. No one is squeezed out of the picture, however important the plans and however small the people concerned.

Nor is that all. Ruth's journey to Bethlehem looks forward to another girl's journey to the same place, where she was to have the baby who would reign over God's worldwide Israel. The city of David, which Ruth and Naomi reached without hope except in God, became the birthplace of the Son of God in whom all the nations would hope. That is why the kings of the world came, at Epiphany, to the city of David—to pay homage to great David's greater Son. In doing so, they followed Ruth exactly, in coming as foreigners to acknowledge Israel's God, Naomi's God, as the one who is sovereign over all human affairs.

They had faith to give their precious gifts to a baby in a poor family. We cannot tell in what strange ways God will work. We *can* be sure that he is utterly worthy of our trust and that he leads us into the dark only to teach us to walk closer to him. We walk by faith, not by sight. But our faith, weak though it is at times, is faith in a great and sovereign God.

17

THE RAINBOW AND
THE PROMISE

WHAT DO YOU FIRST THINK OF when you think of Noah?

Animals? Rain? The ark? The various details added by pious (and sometimes not-so-pious) imagination down the centuries?

I doubt you think of God's covenant. And that is a pity, because the covenant God made with Noah not only shows us the meaning of the original story but also something about God's ways with humans for all time. The covenant with Noah was specifically referred to *all* future generations. What God said to Noah, he says to us.

The background to the covenant is the well-known biblical theme of God's wrath against sin, and his mercy, which carries his people safely through the waves and storms that surround them. The covenant and the promises God then makes arise directly out of the experience of this judgment by flood.

God says, in effect, "I am now making a new start, both for humans and for the whole world." Note, the covenant is not just with Noah and his family, but with all the animals as well and with the earth itself. And as a sign that God means business, he says, "I am hanging up my warrior's bow in the clouds; when you see signs of bad weather you need never be afraid of another judgment by flood."

In other words, from now on the people of God may know for a certainty that even in the midst of wrath there is mercy to be found. The message of Noah's ark—of being carried to safety through the waters of judgment—is thus written as a principle into all God's future dealings with his people and indeed with the whole earth. In the midst of wrath, God remembers mercy. The point of the rainbow is not the trite one that every cloud has a silver lining, nor the futile one that utopia is to be found at the rainbow's end, but the theological one that God, by this sign, gives his solemn assurance to his people in this world that he loves them and will bring them safely through.

It is interesting to see the way this is picked up and amplified in Isaiah 54, which speaks to an oppressed and afflicted people this message of hope:

> In overflowing wrath for a moment
>   I hid my face from you,
> but with everlasting love I will have compassion on you,
>   says the LORD, your Redeemer.

This is like the days of Noah to me:

> Just as I swore that the waters of Noah
>   would never again go over the earth,
> so I have sworn that I will not be angry with you
>   and will not rebuke you.
> For the mountains may depart
>   and the hills be removed,
> but my steadfast love shall not depart from you,
>   and my covenant of peace shall not be removed,
>   says the LORD, who has compassion on you.
>   (Isaiah 54:8-10)

The thrust is: when God's people are downcast and facing impossible or hopeless situations, then they are to look up at the covenant promises of God. This is what Paul is getting at in Romans 8:18 and following. How else could he write that the sufferings of this present time (which for him meant being stoned, beaten, imprisoned, shipwrecked) were not worthy to be compared with the glory which is to be ours? In both passages, as in the Noah story, the whole creation is involved. Isaiah goes on to speak of the fir tree coming up in place of the thorn, and Paul develops the same idea when he talks of the whole creation waiting eagerly for God's children to be glorified (Romans 8:18-21). On that day creation itself will be renewed. God's promise to Noah—that he would not destroy the earth with a flood, that as long as earth remained, summer and winter, seedtime and harvest should not cease—is taken up and transformed into the promise of new life for a tired old world, new life that will be dependent on the new life of God's children, the priests of creation.

Just as the events of Jesus' death and resurrection focus more sharply for us the promises God made to Ruth, so those same events focus the promises to Noah. From now on the people of God may know for a certainty that even in the midst of suffering there is glory to be found—that in the midst of death there is life.

This message too is sealed by God with covenant signs. No ephemeral rainbow: we have the prophetic word made more sure. We too pass through the waters of baptism as we become members of God's people (see Romans 6:2-3; 1 Peter 3:20-22). And Jesus left us a second sign to remind us that we live under God's covenant of life through death. This cup, he said, is the new covenant in my blood. Here we are at the heart of the rainbow. Here is human sin being judged; here is the mercy of God at work to save his people. Here is the promise on which the church rests. Not only the church: this promise too is for the whole creation. Bread and wine, in the Communion service, are taken up into God's purposes and given a meaning that anticipates heaven itself. Here and now, and from day to day, the people of God may know for a certainty that even in the midst of puzzles and problems there is truth and life to be found. That truth and that life has as its pattern none other than the Lord, whom we meet as we break bread together—Jesus Christ, who has given us rest by his sorrow and life by his death.

18

FAITH BEFORE THE TOMB

MARTHA, AS USUAL, WAS IN A BIT of a flap. Mind you, she comes out of this story better than she does out of the one in Luke's Gospel, where she asks Jesus to tell Mary off for not helping her with the housework. But she was still in a flap. "Lord," she says, "if you had been here, my brother would not have died." Later on in the story Mary says exactly the same thing. They had probably said it to each other a hundred times in the four days since Lazarus had died. If only Jesus had been here! Then, true to form, when Jesus does come, it is Martha who dashes out to meet him. "Lord—if only!"

Martha's reaction is right in line with what we all say when something suddenly goes badly wrong. Why didn't God do something about it? Why did it happen to me? What did I do to deserve this? It may be something has cut the ground from under all our well-laid plans—a sudden bereavement, perhaps, as in this story (from John 11). It may be failing a crucial exam, or making a wrong decision in an important situation, or allowing a friendship to go sour on us. Suddenly all our world seems to fall in around us. We all experience Martha's reaction: Lord, if only you had been here to do something about it!

If we are Christians, there are two further things we may well say. Neither of them seems at first to get us very far, but both may in fact be the way toward a solution. The first is seen in the incident of the widow's son whom Elijah raised to life. When the boy died, the widow said to Elijah: "What have you against me, O man of God? You have come to me to bring my sin to remembrance and to cause the death of my son?" (1 Kings 17:18). I don't think this is just pessimism—the attitude of "I suppose it's a judgment on me," which is just another sort of fatalism. Rather, it shows something of a proper humility before God, a recognition that death is the end product of sin, and that therefore, faced with personal suffering or sorrow, we should be ready not to shake our fists at God but to see in earthly troubles a fatherly reminder that without humility, repentance and holiness, death—and more than death—is all we have a right to expect. "Lord, if only you had been here" must on the one hand be tempered with "Lord, I have deserved this, and more."

On the other hand there is a more positive note to be struck. "But even now," says Martha, "I know that God will give you whatever you ask of him" (John 11:22). She is very vague about this, as we may well be. She doesn't even dare to put into explicit words the inarticulate hope that is at the back of her mind. We too, faced with an impossible or hopeless situation, may well feel that all we can do is come to God and put the whole thing into his hands, without being too specific about what we want or expect him to do about it. The widow in the Elijah story saw her bereavement as an occasion for repentance. Martha uses hers as an occasion of faith.

Into this situation comes Jesus, and there follows one of those conversations, so typical of John's Gospel, in which Jesus takes a spark of faith and gently nurses it until it becomes a flame. "Your brother will rise again," he says. "Thank you," replies Martha, not much gratified, "I know that he will rise again in the resurrection on the last day" (John 11:23-24). Martha was quite familiar with the idea of resurrection, and no doubt she, like other mourners, had been reminded of it by those who tried to console her. But the next sentence takes that concept of resurrection and shatters it. Resurrection is not a concept—it's a person. "I am the resurrection and the life," says Jesus. Suddenly Martha is face to face with her abstract notion come to life, and with the future arrived in the present. Her vague hope stands before her in flesh and blood. Then he speaks again.

"Those who believe in me, even though they die, will live, and everyone who lives and believes in me will never die" (John 11:25-26). He points away from Martha's immediate concerns to the big truths involved. Faith in Jesus as the resurrection means that we share the resurrection not only in the future but here and now, under cover of the secrecy of faith. The death we die in repentance is a sharing of Jesus' death, and the life we live in faith (not yet, of course, in sight) is life with him in heaven. "Do you believe this?" Jesus asks Martha.

"Yes, Lord," she replies. "I believe that you are the Messiah, the Son of God, the one coming into the world" (vv. 26-27). And she goes back calmly to the house to tell Mary that Jesus has arrived.

Notice what has happened. Martha came to Jesus so preoccupied with her own terrible situation that she could only see him in the light of that situation—"Lord, if only you'd been here . . . and even now perhaps there's some sort of hope." Jesus accepts her like that, but by the end of the conversation things are very different. When she goes away, she no longer sees Jesus through the haze of her problems. She sees her problems in the light of Jesus. The big problem is still there. Knowing Jesus, she is no longer in a flap about it. Being risen with Christ, we are to seek the things that are above. Life does not suddenly become free of problems, but in the company of the living Christ we may be able to look at them with humility and faith, to cope with them with renewed strength and purpose, and to live our whole lives with holiness and with hope.

19

THOUGH PAINFUL AT PRESENT

WHAT HAPPENS WHEN THE DARKNESS we meet is all our own fault?

It is all very well to talk about faith walking in darkness when God has sent that darkness for some reason. But what happens when the darkness is something we have brought on ourselves? If God appears to be cross, to have hidden from us because of our sin, what should our attitude be then?

The biblical way into this question is to see such darkness as God's way of chastising his people. Chastisement is something that any parent with young children knows all about—or any child of sensible parents. As a father chastises his son, not to make him bitter but to show him how he must behave, so God chastises us. (Deuteronomy 8:5 says as much.) Psalm 94 is devoted to the whole question, and I want to look at it in some detail. I suggest you keep it open as we go—in a modern translation which will bring out the sense of the original fully and clearly.

In this psalm the key verse comes about halfway through: "Happy are those whom you discipline, O Lord" (v. 12). At first sight the subject of disciplining seems to be introduced out of the blue. The first eleven verses are a plea that God will judge the wicked—and hurry up about it (vv. 1-3), a description of how very wicked they are (vv. 4-7) and then a statement of the fact that despite what they think, God knows all about them and their ways (vv. 8-11). Then suddenly there is verse 12. What is it doing here?

The problem the psalmist faces is the problem of opposition. He and other innocent people are suffering at the hands of those who oppose God and his people. It goes on today just as much as it did then. In his case, these might be people outside Israel who are coming over the border and plundering where they can. More probably, though, they are godless people within the nation who are living as practical atheists. That is, they say, "The Lord does not see; the God of Jacob does not perceive [when we take advantage of those who can't stand up for themselves]" (v. 7).

In our case, I suggest that these enemies take various forms. The opposition to God's people and his laws still goes on in the same way; people still take callous advantage of the defenseless, but there is more to it than just that. There are invisible enemies who exercise the same callous tyranny over the people of God: illness, fear, old age, bereavement, temptation, sin. All these things come to us arrogantly (v. 4), claiming that they are the reality and that our belief in God is an illusion (v. 7).

What is faith's reply to this arrogant invasion? Faith goes first to the first truth about God, that he is the almighty maker of heaven and earth. From that fact a few obvious lessons can be drawn. The wicked say that God is asleep or blind or inactive, and in the first three verses of the psalm it almost seems as if the writer is agreeing with them. Rise up, he says—get busy, Lord, these people need punishing, they can't be allowed to get away with it! But when he looks at the facts of who God is, he realizes that it is nonsense to say that God doesn't see all this. The one who made eyes and ears in the first place certainly sees and hears all that is going on. Faith in God as Creator is the bedrock of hope in time of attack.

But verse 10 is the important part: "He who disciplines the nations, . . . does he not chastise?" This verse is moving on from the doctrine of God as Creator to the doctrine of God as moral ruler of the world. He has not only made the world. He doesn't just see and know all that is going on in it. He is actively involved as the moral ruler, the one who is punishing sin and will punish it. Therefore the conclusion follows: this God is not asleep. He isn't looking the other way when things seem to go wrong. On the contrary. Because we know that he is the moral ruler of the world, we know that he works all things together for good to those who love him. Specifically, because we know that he is the one who disciplines the nations, we realize that the oppression and difficulty we suffer is simply God's way of disciplining *us*.

The answer to the question of verse 3 ("How long shall the wicked exult?") is therefore given in verses 12-23. The wicked are being used by God to chastise his own people and teach them patience, and then at the last the wicked will be punished as they deserve. God will judge the wicked when the time is right. In the meantime he is not asleep or ignorant of what is going on, but is actually using the evil in the world to purify his people, to teach them. The psalmist's analysis of what God is doing in verses 8-11 leads naturally into verses 12-13:

> Happy are those whom you discipline, O LORD,
>> and whom you teach out of your law,
> giving them respite from days of trouble,
>> until a pit is dug for the wicked. (Psalm 94:12-13)

When we are suffering, or tempted, or desperate with worry, sorrow or fear, then we tend to say, "Lord, why don't you *do* something?" just like Martha in our last chapter. So verses 1-2 of this psalm: Lord, get up, don't go to sleep! Everything's going wrong!

The reply from God, mirrored here in the psalmist's calm vision of God's just and holy providence over the world, is to this effect: "It is good for you, my child, that you learn to bear with all this; it will teach you patience, because it is loving discipline from me. And you needn't worry about evil, personal or impersonal. The day is coming when it will be rooted out of my world altogether and punished as it deserves."

Once we see this pattern in one place in the Bible it becomes clear that at its heart it is the same all the way through. Here is Joseph, sold into Egypt by his wicked brothers. The effect on Joseph is that it humbles him, trains him and teaches him to rely on God. The effect on the whole family is that in the long run sin is found out. Joseph says to the brothers at the end of Genesis: "Even though you intended to do harm to me, *God intended it for good*" (Genesis 50:20).

Here is Isaiah watching the Assyrians come closer and closer to Jerusalem (chap. 10). He preaches to the Jews that the Assyrians are God's stick with which to beat Israel. Yet when Assyria has done its worst, and God has used the pagan arrogance to chastise Israel, then God will punish Assyria for its pride. God does not cause the sin: he channels it to serve his purposes, and when that is finished he punishes it.

Here is James writing to the young church. "My brothers and sisters, whenever you face trials of any kind, consider it nothing but joy, because you know that the testing of your faith produces endurance; and let endurance have its full effect, so that you may be mature and complete, lacking in nothing" (James 1:2-4).

Here is the writer to the Hebrews: "God is treating you as children; for what child is there whom a parent does not discipline? . . . Now, discipline always seems painful rather than pleasant at the time, but later it yields the peaceful fruit of righteousness to those who have been trained by it" (Hebrews 12:7, 11). Finally, of course, here is God taking all the sin in the world and heaping it on the head of Jesus on the cross. Calvary, the greatest sin in the world, becomes the fountain of every blessing that the world possesses.

So it goes on. God uses the wickedness and folly of the

world as a training ground for his people, out of which to bring good. Because they know that, his people can face the present with patience and the future with hope. One day soon the training will be over, the judgment sin deserves will finally fall, and God's people will be rescued from it fully and forever.

Because we see why chastening comes about, we can also see what it is aiming at— "Blessed is the man . . . whom thou dost teach out of thy law" (Psalm 94:12). Remember Psalm 119:67, 71:

> Before I was humbled I went astray,
> but now I keep your word. . . .
> It is good for me that I was humbled,
> so that I might learn your statutes.

How true that is to our Christian experience! Often it is only when God raps us over the knuckles that we suddenly realize that we are drifting into sin.

Sometimes he does this by letting us see the effects of our sin, on ourselves or on others, to make us loathe it. Sometimes he does it in a sudden event, whether large or small—a road accident, perhaps, or something so trivial as stubbing our toe—and we must be sensitive to feel his discipline when it comes and to be warned off whatever sin it is we are dreaming about or living in. As a father God wants us to live in this hard and difficult world as free, mature sons. He will therefore sometimes allow us to go on a longer rein, to see if we will be obedient even if he doesn't tug us back the instant we stray.

That is what we do with a baby, not a grown son.

But his chastisement—sometimes just his look on us as we read his Word—is meant to be a regular part of our Christian experience until the day when we see him as he is and are finally changed into his likeness. It is meant to prepare us to be more useful in God's service, to train us so that, like gold tested in the fire, we may be more valuable to him, humble enough not to exalt ourselves in the new work he has for us. Through all and in all we have the constant comfort of Psalm 94:14: "The Lord *will not* forsake his people; he will not abandon his heritage."

So we come to the last eight verses of the psalm, which set out the whole sweep of thought gained by the person who sees the wicked on one hand and the unchanging God on the other, and is himself afflicted by the one and comforted by the other.

> Who rises up for me against the wicked?
>> Who stands up for me against evildoers?
> If the Lord had not been my help,
>> my soul would soon have lived in the land of silence.
> When I thought, "My foot is slipping,"
>> your steadfast love, O Lord, held me up.
> When the cares of my heart are many,
>> your consolations cheer my soul.
> Can wicked rulers be allied with you,
>> those who contrive mischief by statute?
> They band together against the life of the righteous,
>> and condemn the innocent to death.
> But the Lord has become my stronghold,

and my God the rock of my refuge.
He will repay them for their iniquity
and wipe them out for their wickedness;
the LORD our God will wipe them out.
(Psalm 94:16-23)

Here is the true position of those who trust God. They do not know what sufferings and problems the next day will bring. All they know is—God.

What do they know of God? That God is a just judge (vv. 1-2). He is the Creator of the world (vv. 8-11), and the sovereign ruler of the world (vv. 10-11). He uses sin and evil to prepare the wicked for judgment and to prepare his people for glory (vv. 12-13). He is the faithful God, who never forsakes his people (vv. 14-15). He is the strengthening God, who holds up his people when they are weak and falling (vv. 16-18). He is the comforting God, who loves and consoles them when there is no other comfort (v. 19). He is the safe stronghold, the sure rock and refuge, in whose care we are safe for all eternity (v. 22). He is the victorious God, who will one day destroy all that has oppressed and terrorized his people (v. 23).

Since this psalm thus turns out to be a tremendous picture of our great God, the God we have been learning about all through this book, we can return and read verse 12 with a new emphasis: "Happy are those whom *you* discipline, O LORD: you who are a God like *this*, loving and sovereign, wise, faithful and true." There is no fear in being disciplined by this God, the triune God—the sovereign Creator and Father, the Son whose sufferings and death lead to our life, the Spirit who is the promised Comforter. When this God disciplines us, he is not vindictive or capricious. We are as safe when we suffer for him as a son in his father's arms.

There is no fear in being disciplined by this God. There is only the certain knowledge that he is loving us enough to make us fully fit for his wonderful presence. This is what John Newton meant when he wrote:

> Since all that I meet shall work for my good,
> The bitter is sweet, the medicine food.
> Though painful at present, 'twill cease before long:
> And then, O how pleasant, the conquerors' song.

20

PIE IN THE SKY?

PART THREE OF THIS BOOK HAS been largely concerned with the way faith turns into hope. Just as love is faith looking at its neighbor, so hope is faith looking at the future. Faith and hope are both contrasted with "sight": compare 2 Corinthians 5:7 ("We walk by faith, not by sight") with Romans 8:24 ("In this hope we were saved. Now hope that is seen is not hope. For who hopes for what is seen?"). We have seen that faith in the almighty God of the Bible looks at the future and knows that it is in God's hands. But what is that future to be? Can we really believe the greatest promise of all—the promise of heaven itself?

One of the most frequent sneers that modern skeptics throw at Christians is that our faith is nothing but a hope for "pie in the sky." They think, and say, that we are so heavenly minded that we are no earthly use. In consequence many Christians have been tempted to soft-pedal any mention of the hope of heaven and to concentrate on the many (very important) aspects of Christianity which speak of this present life, whether it may be of a new dimension to our personal lives or of a new approach to the problems of the world.

But if we are inclined to be embarrassed by the sneer of the skeptic, we will really have our backs to the wall when we hear a chapter like John 14 read in church, as it is in my church around the time of Ascension Day. What are we to make of these "heavenly mansions"? Even if we avoid the old translation and simply call them "heavenly dwelling places," doesn't the whole thing focus attention on heaven in an alarmingly naive and old-fashioned way? Jesus is promising the disciples that he will prepare for them places where they will be able to rest forever—where they will enjoy completely and permanently the relationship with him that has begun on this earth. Isn't this just what the skeptic always suspected? Isn't this a religion that tries to escape this world and life in a perpetual dream of the good things to come? Or—which may be worse—isn't it a faith that dodges all the hardest questions of life by saying, "Never mind, it'll be all right in the end"?

There's enough truth—just enough—in that caricature for it to be recognizable. Ultimately Christians believe that we do not know all the answers in this life, that heaven, when we reach it, will set right the things that are wrong at present; and that, while our present duty is to glorify God by our life in this world, our real desire is, as Paul says, to depart and be with Christ, for that is far better. If we don't have one eye at least fixed on heaven, on its beauty, its joys and its holiness, it may be seriously doubted whether in fact our Christianity is the genuine article. This is one of the great themes of the Ascension. As John Calvin said in his commentary on this passage:

> Christ did not ascend into heaven in a private capacity, to dwell there alone, but rather that it might be the common inheritance of all the godly, and that in this way the head might be united to his members.

If Christ has been raised to heaven, and if we belong to him, then a Christian who is not heavenly minded is no true Christian.

But this in no way means, as the skeptic imagines, that our earthly use is seriously curtailed. Indeed, the Christian doctrine of heaven actually guarantees the opposite. Jesus said to the disciples that they knew where he was going, and they knew the way. Thomas (one commentator describes him as "a loyal but dull disciple") asks the rather obvious question: since they don't know where he is going, how can they know the way? The regal reply Jesus gives—*I am* the way, the truth and the life—is so breathtaking in its implications that most of us, I suspect, water it down to a general pious statement, something like, "Have faith in me, because that's what life is really all about." But we must not gloss over what Jesus actually says. The emphasis of the sentence is on *the way*. What does it mean to say that Jesus is the way to heaven, the way to God—indeed, *the way* to God, since he tells us at once that no one comes to the Father but by him?

The answer shatters any idea that Christian faith gives the

believer a cozy glow that insulates him from the realities of daily life. It is *Jesus* who is the way. Jesus, who was born in a stable. Jesus, who went about doing good, preaching, healing, loving, caring. Jesus, who had nowhere to lay his head, who was despised and rejected by humans. Jesus, who loved his sheep and laid down his life for them. Jesus, who rose, ascended to heaven and is even now preparing the place where his people are to be with him forever. This is the man who says that he is the way. It is this Jesus, not any other, who makes these promises. We must not forget that John 14 is placed not on Easter morning, in the excitement and anticipation of the new life of Jesus and his people. It is spoken on the night Jesus was betrayed. At the very moment when Jesus points us to heaven he also points us to a life of service, of suffering, of holiness, of seeking first the kingdom of God and his righteousness, for ourselves but also for the world. If this is the way, the journey's end is not pie in the sky. That phrase is too ridiculously thin to do justice to the facts. It is glory, true glory, the crown which follows the crown of thorns. It is therefore because we are pointed to heaven so unambiguously that our faith is turned into love, as we are sent out into the world to serve it, following the way Jesus himself went. It is no use watering down the hope of heaven to make it relevant to earth. Only the full-blooded reality of the one will give us relevance to the other.

This means that if we set our hopes on heaven, where Christ is, then (so far from being no earthly use) we have every possible motive not only to reform our lives according to God's holiness but also to live out his love for the whole world. We have a new perspective on our earthly life from which its pains and its puzzles can be seen in their proper light, maybe even to advantage. But if we are embarrassed by the "pie in the sky" sneer and decide to set our minds on earth alone, we have neither the true motive nor the right viewpoint from which to proceed. Those who hope for heaven on earth are continually puzzled because things don't work out that way. Those who know that they follow in Jesus' steps know that they must expect the cross before the glory. Death is at work in us, said Paul, but life in you: Jesus' resurrection is the guarantee that we too shall be raised, and in the meanwhile we are to set our minds on the reality of future glory. As in so many things if we set our minds on heaven, we get earth thrown in. If we put earth first we lose both.

Imagine a boy born blind. From his earliest years he has heard his parents' voices, and he has felt the touch of their hands. He knows them, but has never had any of the hundreds of joys of seeing them. He has never seen the look in his father's eye or the smile on his mother's face. Imagine this boy then having an operation, so that for the first time he can see them. Imagine the bandages being taken off and his eyes meeting those of his parents for the first time. That, I suggest, is something of what heaven will be like. Here we know in part, we walk by faith and not by sight. We live our lives in obedient, trusting faith, hearing the Father's voice and knowing something of his love. One day the bandages will be off, and then we shall realize that this faith, focused in God's chosen signs and particularly in the Lord's Table, has been all along a real foretaste of heaven. For the moment Jesus' message to us is: "Do not let your hearts be troubled. Believe in God, believe also in me" (John 14:1).

We are therefore, to change the picture, like people who are trying to find their way into the center of a maze. The true path requires us very often to take what appears to be the wrong way to the middle. What looks the quickest way will get us hopelessly lost. But we have an advantage. We have a guide who has gone before, who knows the way and who has left us his footprints to follow. They lead along a difficult path, to be sure. But just in case we lose heart and begin to imagine that there never was such a guide, or that there must surely be an easier way than this, or that there never was a middle to the maze anyway, we are given in John 14, and in the ascension of Jesus, a glimpse, a sudden sight over the hedges, of our guide himself safely arrived at his destination. And that sight, by en-couraging us to press on to join him, tells us once again that it is in his footsteps that, by faith, we must walk. Our faith may be small. Jesus reveals to us the greatness of God and the cer-tainty of his love.

Scripture Index

Other InterVarsity Press Resources from N. T. Wright

The Challenge of Jesus
N. T. Wright offers clarity and a full accounting of the facts of the life and teachings of Jesus, revealing how the Son of God was also solidly planted in first-century Palestine. *978-0-8308-2200-3, 202 pages, hardback*

Resurrection
This 50-minute DVD confronts the most startling claim of Christianity—that Jesus rose from the dead. Shot on location in Israel, Greece and England, N. T. Wright presents the political, historical and theological issues of Jesus' day and today regarding this claim. Wright brings clarity and insight to one of the most profound mysteries in human history. Study guide included. *978-0-8308-3435-8, DVD*

Evil and the Justice of God
N. T. Wright explores all aspects of evil and how it presents itself in society today. Fully grounded in the story of the Old and New Testaments, this presentation is provocative and hopeful; a fascinating analysis of and response to the fundamental question of evil and justice that faces believers. *978-0-8308-3398-6, 176 pages, hardback*

Evil
Filmed in Israel, South Africa and England, this 50-minute DVD confronts some of the major "evil" issues of our time—from

tsunamis to AIDS—and puts them under the biblical spotlight. N. T. Wright says there is a solution to the problem of evil, if only we have the honesty and courage to name it and understand it for what it is. Study guide included. *978-0-8308-3434-1, DVD*

Justification: God's Plan and Paul's Vision

In this comprehensive account and defense of the crucial doctrine of justification, Wright also responds to critics who have challenged what has come to be called the New Perspective. Ultimately, he provides a chance for those in the middle of and on both sides of the debate to interact directly with his views and form their own conclusions. *978-0-8308-3863-9, 279 pages, hardback*

Colossians and Philemon

In Colossians, Paul presents Christ as "the firstborn over all creation," and appeals to his readers to seek a maturity found only in Christ. In Philemon, Paul appeals to a fellow believer to receive a runaway slave in love and forgiveness. In this volume N. T. Wright offers comment on both of these important books. *978-0-8308-4242-1, 199 pages, paperback*

N. T. Wright for Everyone Bible Study Guides

The guides in this series covering each book of the New Testament are designed to help readers understand Scripture in fresh ways under the guidance of one of the world's leading biblical scholars. Thoughtful questions, prayer suggestions and useful background and cultural information all guide you or a group more deeply into God's Word. They can be used on their own or alongside Wright's New Testament for Everyone commentaries. Discover how you can participate more fully in God's kingdom. *19 volumes, paperback*